# Quantum Christianity

## Bringing Science and Religion Together for the New Millennium

## Jim Groves

MountainDoor Books
Seattle
quantumxpian@gmail.com

Published by MountainDoor Books

ISBN-13: 978-0615493374
ISBN: 0615493378

# FOR PATTY

Who constantly teaches me that there are more things in heaven and earth than are dreamt of in my philosophy.

# CONTENTS

# PART III: GOD IN THE DETAILS ................................. 77

## Quantum Theology ..........................................................................79

## Finding God in the Ambiguous Universe:
## Surrendering Our Certitude .........................................................81

## Finding God in the Uncertain Universe:
## The Elusiveness of God .................................................................84

## Finding God in the Probabilistic Universe:
## Playing the Odds ...........................................................................87

## Finding God in the Empirical Universe:
## The Fundamental Role of Consciousness .......................................88

## Finding God in the Entangled Universe:
## Rethinking Omnipresence ............................................................91

## Finding God in the Holographic Universe:
## Tying It All Together .....................................................................93

# PART IV: QUANTUM THEORY AND CHRISTIAN
# THEOLOGY ......................................................................... 97

## The Nature of God ........................................................................99

# INTRODUCTION

*Anyone who is not shocked by quantum theory
has not understood it. — Physicist Niels Bohr*

I'm not really qualified to write this book. Heck, I'm barely qualified to *read* it. But that's part of why I wrote it in the first place. There are more than a few books on science and theology, but they tend to be weighty volumes meant to impress scholars, not to help ordinary people resolve the tensions between their scientific and religious beliefs. Most books that relate modern physics to religion do so by talking about Eastern religions like Buddhism. As far as I know, there's no book that takes both physics and Christianity seriously, *and* that does so in a way that people like you and me can understand.

And so that's why I had to write this book, because no one else had written it, and I wasn't sure that anyone would. Besides, I thought that I had at least a little something to contribute along these lines. I have a Master of Divinity degree from a reputable seminary (which I won't name so they can *stay* reputable) and spent almost three years as a Presbyterian minister. Then I became a technical writer for a well-known computer company (ditto). To make sure that my nerdiness was not limited to hardware and software, I continued to exercise my biblical aptitude by teaching Sunday school and tried to keep my lunchtime reading list as broad as possible.

That's what led me to *The Physics of Consciousness* by Evan Harris Walker. This book, a compelling mixture of quantum mechanical theory, Zen Buddhism, and personal reminiscences, started me on the path of questioning both my understanding of what science tells us about the world and what traditional Christianity tells us about God. I learned that the universe is not a precisely engineered machine, but a roiling cauldron of innumerable random and sometimes weird events. I also realized that the common image of God as an old, bearded man surfing the clouds, even when abstracted to something along the lines of a Great Spirit motif, couldn't really mesh with the picture of reality painted by quantum theory.

That led me to further reading on the subject, and the Reading List at the end of the book tells you about the books I found most useful. The one thing that struck me about most of those books, though, is how dauntingly opaque they are. A few of them had so much advanced theory (for me, at least) that I had to skip over whole sections just to keep my head from exploding. And even though many of them looked at the religious repercussions of quantum theory, they did so in the context of Eastern religions that talk about a world that is, at its core, just an illusion. It's a lot more difficult to talk about Christian faith in the context of a description of reality that doesn't fit the notion of a creator spinning the universe into being like a potter working clay on his wheel. So I decided to accept the challenge of writing a book that tries to do so, even if I'm not the best qualified person for the job. If that person would kindly step forward, I'll be more than happy to hand over the responsibility to them.

Then again, even though I'm undoubtedly not *the* best qualified, perhaps I'm qualified enough. While I lack the certifiable scientific and theological chops that would make this book both informative and credible, I at least have 20-some-odd years' experience as a professional communicator that has taught me the importance of writing to my audience, a skill that most scholars notoriously lack. So possibly I understand the subject matter just well enough to interpret it for readers who have just a little less understanding but are seeking to gain more.

So, Gentle Reader, the book you hold in your hand isn't intended to overwhelm your skepticism with footnotes and formulas, much less to use them as a device to prove the existence of God or the fundamental truth of the Christian faith. Rather, it's my hope to give you a taste of the frankly bizarre universe portrayed by quantum physics and to show how the very nature of that bizarre universe actually leaves room for God's existence and activity in a way that classical science could not. Finally, I want to take a fresh look at the Christian faith in light of those insights and consider which traditional beliefs can be sustained and which must be radically redrawn.

In the end, I pray that you will approach this book with an open mind. If you do, even if it doesn't change your opinions, at least it will give you the opportunity to better understand your beliefs and how they are being challenged by the a scientific worldview you probably didn't learn much about in school. That's really all that I ask of this book, and I hope you will, too.

I'd like to add a brief note about the language I used to refer to God. Although my time in seminary and other corners of Christianity has made me sensitive to the problems that come from using masculine language (he, his, him) to refer to God, and even though I really don't believe God is somehow more male than female, I deliberately chose to use masculine language to talk about God. I did so because, frankly, I didn't want my refusal to use traditional language to become a stumbling block for those of you who haven't yet adapted to a more gender-neutral view of God. Even more important, as I talked about God in the light of quantum physics, I found that the portrayal of God sometimes became so abstract that it began to verge on turning a personal God into a *thing*. That wasn't my intention, so I continued to use personal pronouns (which, in English, are unavoidably gender specific) to struggle against that tendency. To those who are put off by the results of that decision, I apologize.

# PART I: THE PROBLEM OF FAITH IN THE MODERN WORLD

## Culture Wars: Faith vs. Reason

About 45 years ago, a *Time* magazine cover asked, "Is God Dead?" More recently, a report delivered to a meeting of the American Physical Society meeting in Dallas, no less, declared that an analysis of census information in nine countries indicated that religion would soon be "extinct" in those locations.

Faith in God is at an all-time low, especially in places that are actually part of the modern world, like Western Europe. Polls show that only a small fraction of people in Western Europe believe in God, and the same is true in places like Japan, where the religious traditions never were very strong on belief in a Supreme Being in the first place.

Wherever you look, the people who have the highest education are the least likely to believe in God, and those who have little or no formal education have the greatest faith in God. It would appear that the more you know, the harder it is for you to see how God can exist. Or to put it another way, it seems that faith and ignorance go together like a horse and carriage and are just as unfashionable.

Americans don't fit this trend, however. Although the average American has a higher level of education than in most countries, more of us believe in God than people living in places just about anywhere except predominantly Muslim countries. But in America, even though just about everyone says that they believe in God, our faith is pretty shallow. Overall, the number of

Americans who attend church regularly is lower now than just about any time in the last century, and when they are asked by pollsters, twice as many people claim to attend church regularly than actually do. Even before the twentieth century, church attendance was really quite low, even though most Americans think that our forefathers and foremothers were an especially pious bunch.

Today, our personal piety is also pretty thin. Despite all the arguments about prayer in schools and other civic places, few Americans actually pray every day, at least not very earnestly. (Sorry, but I don't think "God is great, God is good..." or "Now I lay me down to sleep..." represents heartfelt piety.) A lot of Americans say that they think the Ten Commandments should be posted on courthouse lawns and in public schoolrooms, but if asked, disturbingly few of those same Americans would be able to name more than four or five easy ones, such as thou shalt not kill, steal, or commit adultery. Most of those same Americans would be upset to see the return of the so-called blue laws that kept stores closed on Sundays a few decades ago and would think them a violation of their God-given right to sell and shop whenever they want. Anymore, even the most hard-nosed fundamentalists don't think twice about stopping at the Piggly Wiggly on their way home from church.

Even in one of the most supposedly religious countries in the world, religious faith doesn't seem to penetrate very deep into people's public lives. Think about it: When was the last time you saw someone pausing to say grace over a Big Mac? Most of us think that such public displays of devotion are odd, maybe even downright peculiar, and so even the most devout people adjust their public behavior to conform to the prevailing secular standard.

For a country that thinks itself very religious, we're surprisingly narrow-minded about other people's religiousness. The vast majority of times when religious people appear in a TV show or movie, they're shown as buffoons, hypocrites, or dangerous fanatics. Some people might say that this is just because Hollywood is run by a cynical, profane elite, but this argument is pretty weak. After all, when other kinds of bigotry have appeared on the screen, protests have swiftly persuaded media executives to tone it down or get rid of it altogether. Racial and ethical stereotypes are not allowed unless they are being lampooned. And yet two types of people who can still be ridiculed are the religious and the overweight. (As a member of both groups, I feel especially picked on.) If even a small minority of the American audience was serious enough about religion to be offended by such portrayals, they would be off our screens faster than you can say the *N* word.

Even in private, few people spend much of their time being religious. Maybe most families have a Bible (hopefully not one with the word *Gideons* embossed on the front), but not many Americans actually read it regularly. Few families make it a point to pray together, except maybe at mealtime, and fewer still try to give their children even a basic religious education.

If anything, the state of religion in our common political life is even worse. Our leaders feel like they have to claim to be pious Christians (or in a handful of cases, pious Jews), but our government hardly shows the influence of real Judeo/Christian values. Oh, there's a lot of trumpeting about a "culture of life," but the same leaders who make the most noise about it have pushed us into wars that have caused the deaths of thousands of innocent civilians. Why is it that "What Would Jesus Do?" seems limited to matters of personal morality but somehow never affects our foreign and social policy? Or does anyone think that Jesus would start a war against *anyone*, much less a preemptive war against a far-off nation that posed no imminent threat to us? Or does anyone think that Jesus would push cuts in programs that care for the poor and disabled to pay for tax cuts for the rich? When did Jesus ever say anything nice about the rich or tell the poor that they deserved scorn for their condition? (Sorry. I couldn't help letting the pissed-off preacher in me come out.)

I think it's clear that our country really doesn't care about how sincere our leaders are in their religious beliefs, just as long as they seem to agree with our own narrow and self-centered worldview. Otherwise, how can we explain how evangelicals lined up against arguably the first born-again President (Jimmy Carter) to help elect a candidate who was the first divorced President (Ronald Reagan), all in the name of "family values"? The truth is that the majority of Americans don't really care that much about our leaders' real beliefs, just so long as what the candidate *claims* to believe is able to gain the support of a small-but-powerful religious minority with enough money and influence to tilt an election their way.

And so we find ourselves in a nation that is pretty much *superficially* religious, a nation whose citizens rarely let what little faith they have affect their actions and who make fun of those who do.

As we become more separated from our religious roots, we find ourselves cut off from the values that gave us a strong foundation for our lives. Our lives become more and more empty and meaningless and we end up trying to fill that emptiness with *things* that we think will make us happy. Instead of honoring people whose lives reflect virtue and integrity, we most admire people who are rich and famous, without really caring how they got that way. The quickest path to celebrity is being notorious, and while we might give the Paris Hiltons of the world a cursory "tsk tsk," we still give them more attention and admiration then we do to people who actually achieve something important. The people we think are successful are those who look good, who get (or are born) rich, and who are able to keep their faces on the cover of *People* magazine.

To make things even worse, though, we export this cultural toxic waste around the world through our media and consumer-obsessed corporations. Try to imagine how our movies and TV shows, filled with partial nudity, extramarital sex, and openly gay people is received among people who think that a woman is indecent when she shows her face in public. It's easy to see why there's a fundamentalist backlash in the Muslim world against us. I hate to admit it, but there's a good reason why they call us the Great Satan: In the Bible, Satan is the tempter, and we are certainly tempting much of the rest of the world to abandon their traditional values so they can imitate our casual self-indulgence and profanity.

Naturally, the Muslim world isn't the only place where a fundamentalist backlash is taking place. America has a sizable fundamentalist movement, too. Even though Christian fundamentalism represents a small minority of Americans, it's a very vocal movement that is able to shape people's opinions even if it's not able to convert them to its core beliefs. As a result, a sizable chunk of Americans think that evolution and global warming are still controversial among scientists and that the Bible can be used like a textbook to answer questions about biology, geology, and history. Without a doubt, this is because Americans feel that society is changing just too damn fast, and so they nostalgically cling to a Golden Age when everybody's faith had a firm foundation in God's excellent Word. Not that people really want to go back to the way things were a hundred years ago, but they do miss what they like to imagine were the solid virtues of the past.

But religious people aren't the only fundamentalists, of course. There's also a scientific fundamentalism that is at least as influential as religious fundamentalism because of the way it controls how scientists go about their business and because of how it shapes what educators do, especially at the college level. Believe it or not, scientific fundamentalism is even less tolerant than religious fundamentalism because, while religious fundamentalists have to accept at least a part of the scientific worldview (mainly because it works so well), scientific fundamentalists think that they have to reject the entire

religious worldview. For the most part, religious fundamentalists are at least willing to admit the truth of the
ideas of Galileo, Newton, Mendel, and Einstein—in fact,
practically all scientific pioneers except for Darwin and
his heirs—but scientific fundamentalists crusade against
all religious faith, even to the point of rejecting belief in a
generic, impersonal, uninvolved God. The scientific
community usually treats with contempt those few
scientists who have the courage to even suggest that
there might be any reality beyond what can be proven by
experiments. These scientists find it hard to get their
works published and to get funding or associates for
their research, even when that research has nothing to do
with religion. It's no surprise, then, that most scientists
who do manage to keep some sort of religious faith hide
it from their colleagues rather than risk crippling their
careers.

The problem for the rest of us is that all kinds of fundamentalism are totalitarian. That is, they delude themselves into thinking that they provide the only correct
answers to *all* questions and so they insist that everyone
must adopt their particular beliefs and none other. For
most of us, scientism (the religion of science) is especially
attractive because its practitioners are so useful to us.
After all, science is the source of all of the medical won-
ders and technological gizmos that make our way of life
possible. And it's hard to argue with the claims of scientism when science has shown itself to be so successful at
figuring out how the world really works. The problem is
that while science is really good at answering the question *How?*, it's completely unable to answer the deeper

question *Why?*, a question it doesn't even think is important.

So most of us find ourselves stuck between these two militant factions. For the most part, we agree with the scientific worldview because it's so reliable. Science tells us that natural laws, not God, control the universe, and since we hardly ever see true miracles that defy those laws, it's hard to argue with science on that point. On the other hand, we can't completely surrender to scientism because it can't give our lives meaning and direction. Even though our everyday experience doesn't really jibe with religion's emphasis on the supernatural, at least religion is better at helping us find the meaning and direction that scientism just plain ignores.

As we'll see next, the scientific worldview is the one that we live by day to day. We almost always trust reason, not revelation, as the way to understand how the world works, even when reason seems to push our spiritual needs to the fringe of our lives.

## The Role of Science in Western Culture

The ultimate irony of the debate between science and faith is that the argument is already over, and science has won. The scientific worldview has conquered all others, at least in America and the more modern parts of the world. It's everywhere, influencing practically everything we do. Seriously. Planning a party? Do you ask your pastor to say a prayer to beg God not to rain on your event? Or instead do you check your favorite weather report to find out what the odds of fair weather are for your special day? The fact that the second approach is the only one just about any of us would seriously consider shows how much of what we believe is based on science, not on religion. We no longer believe that weather is caused by the whim of a fickle God who can be coaxed to do what we want, but rather that it is the result of natural forces that scientists can measure and predict the effects of. Even the most religious among us watch the weather report to plan our day, not to laugh at how impertinent it is.

Or think of what we do when someone we love is critically injured. If we're not Christian Scientists, we call 911 or rush them to the hospital, *then* we might pray for God to get involved, often asking him to help the doctors and nurses practice their science well. In a way, we've managed to demote God to the role of physician's assistant.

Every day, we do things that people a few generations ago would have thought impossible, mainly because science has shown that it can be done. We climb aboard an airplane and, despite its great weight, we trust that it will lift off and fly us to where we're going. We watch events happening on the other side of the planet, probably unaware that the picture is being carried by satellites and lasers over glass "wires." We point our phones at an interesting scene, record a video, and then send it to five friends around the country. Each of these activities began with scientific theory that was confirmed by experiments and then applied to technology. The only way this technology is possible is because of how well the scientific process has been able to give us a deeper understanding of how our world works.

Although we are not aware of it—and in fact, we probably would deny it—we in the Western world have come to believe more firmly in Isaac Newton than in God. We go about our days assuming that the physical rules that Newton discovered control how the world around us will behave, in part because those rules have been declared to be laws that seem to be more reliable than any of God's moral laws. We understand that things fall when we let go of them, not just out of habit or because of supernatural forces pulling them down, but because they are obeying a law of gravitation that Newton said controls the whole universe. When we feel how hard it is to move something heavy, we know that Newton's law of momentum explains why it's so difficult, not that the darn thing is just being stubborn. Even though we may be only vaguely aware of how Newton's ideas came to be accepted as laws (by first being worked out as mathematical formulas that were then verified by countless experiments), we have come to accept their authority without quibble. On the other hand, when someone is caught doing something bad, even something truly evil, the best we can do is pray that justice will be done, and usually we assume that it is up to us as a society to make sure that it is.

The place that Newton holds in our culture is mainly because he stood at the beginning of the scientific revolution that came to define how we look at the world. Newton's theories were among the first to be systematically tested, both by analyzing the math behind them and through scientific experimentation. This turned into a virtuous cycle of sorts, where the truth of Newton's groundbreaking insights was ever more firmly supported and the process of scientific experimentation itself came to be increasingly accepted as the most reliable way of revealing the truth. What happened as a result was the birth of the Enlightenment, when Western society turned away forever from blind obedience to authority and turned instead to the scientific method as the most trusted path to knowledge. In the Christian world, even the Bible became the subject of scientific study by scholars, scholars who often reached conclusions that disturbed the faithful and sparked a backlash against using science to study things that should be kept securely within church walls.

In spite of this limited backlash, though, even the most religious people in America accept the basic validity of the methods and assumptions of scientists. Yes, some people are offended by certain scientific theories because those theories seem to deny something that they believe God revealed through the Bible—in effect, calling God a liar—and yet those same people will often try to use other scientific theories to disprove the ones they disagree with. For example, fundamentalist Christians who think that Darwin's theory of evolution contradicts the story of the creation of life in the book of Genesis will often claim that Newton's laws of entropy prove that evolution is impossible. After all, they say, Newton's laws say that everything is moving from order to disorder, so evolution must be impossible because the new life forms that supposedly result from evolution are usually more complex than the ones that came before. These "proofs" rarely stand up to close examination, though, because they almost always twist these laws or just flat out apply them wrongly. Even so, the fact that fundamentalists attempt to use science to discredit science shows how much the scientific point of view is actually accepted by people who, if asked, would heatedly deny that their worldview depends more on science than on revelation.

## The Scientific Method and Truth

One really important reason that the scientific worldview has taken over Western culture, despite feeble resistance by believers, is because the method it uses is so successful at figuring out what is true and what is false. And it is successful because, unlike other ways to seek truth and describe reality, it is truly progressive. Before the scientific method took charge, Truth was handed down by people with authority. And because we didn't have bumper stickers back then to tell us to, we didn't question authority. So, if you believed that everything that Aristotle wrote was true, you wouldn't look for evidence that his worldview was flawed precisely because it was your worldview as well. No wonder people thought that reality couldn't change.

On the other hand, the scientific view of the world is based on the idea that whatever we think is true is only partial and ever-changing. Every discovery, no matter how firmly supported and widely accepted, is assumed to be just one step on a journey, one piece of an always-growing puzzle. So even when a theory is "proved" (a term scientists don't like to use, except maybe when talking down to us laypeople), it simply becomes the basis for new hypotheses. On the other hand, hypotheses that aren't confirmed by experiments are thrown out, and scientists who continue to cling to them are pushed to the margins of the scientific community and lose its respect.

Because of this forward-moving quality, the scientific method gets better and better at predicting the future, that is, what develops from current conditions and events. This is most often seen in the laboratory, of course, but it also applies to everyday happenings as well. The weather report is the most obvious example of this, but such areas as medicine and engineering are also based largely on the ability of the scientific method to predict an outcome even when the exact conditions and events leading to that outcome have never been seen before.

Even beyond these everyday examples, science was able to predict such (literally) earth-shaking developments as the splitting of the atom long before they were accomplished. Newton, much less prophets and philosophers, couldn't have foreseen such a discovery, but the scientific method that Newton pioneered created the conditions that eventually led to the theories that resulted in nuclear fission. In other words, scientists didn't just stumble upon nuclear fission. Instead, the ideas of such visionaries as Albert Einstein led scientists to perform experiments that, through the process of constant fine-tuning, enabled them to create the first controlled nuclear reaction and then, sadly, the uncontrolled nuclear reaction of the atomic bomb.

Such developments as these have led us to give the scientific method a level of authority far greater than any other. Maybe with the exception of the most willfully closed-minded religious believers, we have come to view science as the most reliable way of finding the truth, the most consistent and powerful way to learn how the world really works. While we may embrace scraps of our ancestors' faith, the reality is that we place far more trust in scientists than we do in prophets and priests, at least on a day-to-day basis.

## Technology as the Fruits of Science

Up to this point, I've talked about the impact of science on our lives in terms that are pretty abstract and obscure. Even though we may vaguely grasp the way science shows us how the atom works or how the universe began, that understanding has little to do with how we go about our daily routine. In fact, though, science plays a key role in almost every moment of each day because of the critical role that science has played in the creation of the technology that defines how we live in the modern world. Because we recognize this relationship, our dependence on technology gives greater strength to the authority of science in our minds.

A revolution began at the end of the nineteenth century when science was applied more and more to the creation of new technology. Before that time, advances in technology were mostly evolutionary, the result of practical experimentation: New things were tried and, if they turned out to improve how something worked, they continued to be used. If they didn't, then they were discarded. Although this sounds a lot like the scientific method, it is different because it was purely a trial-and-error process. The goal was to make the thing itself better, not to learn about the basic principles of nature that allowed the new thing to work. For this reason, invention was more craft than science, that is, the pursuit of knowledge for its usefulness, not for its own sake. Even the best-known inventor, Thomas Edison, developed most of his products through trial and error instead of applying scientific theory. His famous saying that invention is one percent inspiration and ninety-nine percent perspiration shows this: There's no mention of any use of scientific theory, just new ideas and effort.

In a way, Edison was among the last of the "old-school" inventors. As advanced scientific knowledge began to flower in the nineteenth and early twentieth centuries (Einstein published his first paper in 1905), the discoveries that resulted began to be used to improve old technologies and to create new ones. This trend was not entirely new, of course. After all, Benjamin Franklin studied the nature of lightening and showed that it is a flow of electricity, so he was able to invent the lightning rod as a way to safely channel the electricity from the air to the ground through a wire instead of through the building itself. But this way of applying scientific discovery to the art of invention continued to be more the exception than the rule until the twentieth century.

Physical theories of electricity and magnetism inspired the greatest results among inventors at the beginning of the twentieth century. Early nineteenth-century scientists like Michael Faraday, Luigi Galvani, Alessandro Volta, André-Marie Ampère, and Georg Simon Ohm developed the scientific knowledge of electromagnetism that was the foundation for technologies created by later nineteenth-century engineers such as Nikola Tesla (electric motors), George Westinghouse and Thomas Edison (electrical generation and transmission), Samuel Morse (the telegraph), and Alexander Graham Bell (the telephone), and in the following century, such inventions as radio, the vacuum tube, and the cathode ray tube used in the first TVs and computer monitors.

Electronic gizmos are the most obvious product of science, but just about every invention of the twentieth century was at least helped along by science. For example, the Wright Brothers' knowledge of the Bernoulli Principle (the unequal pressure that gives wings their lift and propellers their thrust) made it possible for them to invent the airplane. The theories of James Clerk Maxwell and Ludwig Boltzmann led to the invention of refrigeration. And on and on.

Most of us are at least vaguely aware of how the scientific method has sped up the development of the technology that we use every day, and this helps give the scientific process a greater credibility than can be found in any other area of human activity. Religion, on the other hand, appears regressive by comparison because it is mostly based on the authority of writings and traditions from the ancient past. It's no surprise, then, that as technology becomes more and more central to the way we live, religion is losing its influence, receding to the background and fading in importance.

## Material Realism

So science has taken over Western culture by infiltrating itself through the technology that saturates our experience. But how, exactly, has science shaped our belief systems in a way that undermines our belief in God?

At the heart of the scientific view of the world is a philosophy known as *material realism*. I call it a philosophy because even though its ideas are the basis of science, material realism is basically a religious claim that cannot be proven by any method, scientific or otherwise. Instead, the scientific method starts with material realism and creates its rules assuming that material realism is true. More to the point, as we shall see later, when scientists happen to stumble upon results that challenge material realism, those results (and often the scientists who discover them) are almost automatically dismissed as being unscientific.

Material realism is the belief that reality is just the physical (material) world and that all you need to know to understand everything is the physical laws that govern the material world. According to material realism, talk about a "higher" reality is not only unnecessary, it's a useless distraction that gets in the way of scientific progress.

As Amit Goswami explains in his book, *The Self-Aware Universe*, there are five dominant principles that form the basis of the philosophy of material realism, principles that just about everyone with any sort of modern education accepts to some degree or other. These five principles are *strong objectivity, causal determinism, locality, physical* (or *material*) *monism,* and *epiphenomenalism.* I'll try to translate.

*Strong objectivity* is the belief that reality is, well, real. That is, it's the belief that reality does not need someone to observe events for them to happen. It is a belief system that answers the question, "If a tree falls in a forest and no one hears it, does it make a sound?" with an emphatic *Yes!* Strong objectivity says that the structures and processes of reality don't have to be observed to exist and affect each other. They are not subjective (dependent on the viewpoint of an observer), but rather objective (independent of any observer). When you get down to it, this is the whole reason scientists follow the scientific method in the first place, to find out what is really real, not just what they expect to see. Scientists believe that, to quote *The X Files,* "the truth is out there," waiting to be uncovered. According to strong objectivity, that's all that science does: uncover the truth that is there but hidden. This belief has been such a basic part of the worldview of scientists that most have not even considered the possibility that it might be wrong, even when—as we will see in Part II—some of the discoveries of quantum physicists have challenged it. In a way, it's easy to understand why that might be the case. Strong objectivity is such a basic part of the way scientists look at the world that to question it is to challenge their entire worldview. Pretty scary stuff.

*Causal determinism* is another basic belief that is essential to the scientific worldview. At heart, it is the assumption that things don't just happen spontaneously, that every event has a finite set of causes that would produce the same result every time so long as you could exactly reproduce those causes. Of course, every event in the real world is the result of a very complex combination of preconditions that is practically impossible to recreate, but this fact is thought to be just due to our human limitations, not a flaw in the belief itself. A logical consequence of this view, of course, is that there's no such thing as true randomness, so that even events that look random—like a coin toss or a throw of the dice—can be explained by the conditions and forces that produce what *seems* to be a random event. In other words, it's not really a matter of chance that a coin lands heads up, for example. Instead, in theory you could explain it by the amount and direction of the force you used to flip the coin, any imbalances in the weight of the coin, the influence of air currents, and the surface that the coin lands on. According to causal determinism, then, if you could exactly reproduce those conditions, the coin would land heads up every time. Of course, this is how the scientific method is supposed to work: The scientist controls all of the conditions of an experiment except one. By changing that one condition (called the *variable*) and seeing the differences in outcome that result, the scientist can figure out how changes in the variable produce different outcomes. This makes sense only if the scientist believes that each outcome is exclusively the result of the events and conditions that lead up to that outcome, that the result is no more and no less than the sum of the parts that produced it. Again, however, the discoveries of quantum physics challenge the idea that this principle applies at all levels of reality.

*Locality* means that everything is, well, where it is. While that might seem ridiculously obvious, it really isn't. Not only does this mean that things are bound to their particular location, more importantly, it means that the influence that one thing—be it a material object or an energy field—has over another thing is limited to its place and time.

In some ways, this might actually be harder for us to believe than it would have been a hundred years ago. In this age of telecommunications, we constantly encounter experiences that make it seem that events can affect other events far away. For example, we watch TV, seeing things that are happening hundreds of miles away. What isn't apparent, though, is that even though a television set can display an image captured far away from us, this happens because that image is turned into radio waves that travel between the TV station and the TV set. The distance in space (and time) is spanned by events that are set in motion at the TV station and, in effect, spread as a series of events (radio waves) that eventually reach the TV set and cause the picture to be displayed there. So the appearance that an event causes a result at a distance is really an illusion, the product of a chain of events extending unbroken from the original cause to the eventual result.

The principle of locality is essential to the scientific worldview because we need it to understand the chain of cause and effect of causal determinism. If an event at location A causes something to happen at location B, the principle of causal determinism means that you have to be able to explain the chain of events that take place between A and B. The principle of locality is so essential to the scientific method, in fact, that when theories of quantum mechanics showed that—at the subatomic level, at least—events in one location *can* affect events at a distance without things happening in between, Albert Einstein spent much of his later years trying unsuccessfully to prove that those theories were wrong.

*Physical monism* is the idea that the physical (material) world is all that there is, that there's no reality apart from the physical processes that we are a part of. By definition, this rules out anything metaphysical, from the human soul to God himself, at least to the extent that either the soul or God can affect or even be seen from the physical world. Everything that does happen can (and must) be explained by the laws of physics. Anything that doesn't play by those rules is, well, unthinkable. If we admit that the metaphysical might be possible, we also must admit that science cannot give us a satisfactory explanation for everything. Most of us can live with this incongruity, but the scientific fundamentalist is horrified by this possibility. And yet, on this point, we might be able to find a way of affirming physical monism in a way that embraces (and explains) notions of reality that would usually be described in metaphysical terms. In fact, this is what this book is all about.

*Epiphenomenalism* tries to apply the other scientific principles to the fact that we human beings are conscious, a fact that is extremely hard to explain using those scientific principles. Even though we experience our own consciousness as the essence of who we are, scientists usually conclude that consciousness is only a byproduct (epiphenomenon) of the biological processes of our nervous systems. To a certain extent, we accept this conclusion. We see that when someone's brain is injured, that person's consciousness can be reduced or even wiped out. We count on having our consciousness suppressed when we are given anesthesia for surgery, and we are glad when we awake afterwards with no memory of what happened. And yet we have the unshakable feeling that there is something more primary, more durable at the center of our consciousness than anything that can be explained by anatomy and physiology. This actually may provide the best explanation for our persistent belief in a supernatural level of reality that can't be explained away by science. Even scientists who insist that there's no other explanation can't help but act as though they are motivated by something beyond the principles of material realism, as though they have freedom of choice and that their choices are meaningful, that *Why?* really is as important as *How?*.

Despite this very personal experience of a metaphysical reality that goes against the principles of material realism and the rest, we in Western cultures have become so completely programmed with the ideas and values of science that they have come to control how we think, even if we're not scientists ourselves. Indeed, to a certain extent, material realism has become one of the fundamentals of Western *religion* because Western religion describes God first and foremost as the one who created the material world. Of course, Western religious traditions insist that a metaphysical dimension does exist, but they also consider the physical realm to be highly significant, very much real. This is in contrast to Eastern religions like Hinduism and Buddhism that insist that the material world is just an illusion. In the West, though, we believe that the material world that God created is, to a certain extent, self-sufficient. And so we live out our lives firmly convinced that the physical world is what is truly real.

Of course, most of us still believe in miracles, but even there, our belief in miracles is based on the idea that the material world is pretty much self-contained and governed by laws that make it predictable. Miracles occur when the unpredictable happens, when God intervenes from outside to suspend the laws of nature that make the world stable, that make it an acceptable reality. It's exactly because God so rarely interferes with the material world that we can count on it to be trustworthy and constant.

## Science and God's Place in the Universe

We have reached the point where the material world is more real to us than any spiritual dimension, and the scientific worldview has come to dominate how we approach the world. In modern societies, even among those who are most religious, our assumption is that any new insights into the way the world works will come through the scientific process, not through supernatural revelation. We explain things that happen around us by using scientific, not religious, concepts. The sun doesn't rise because some divine power is moving it, but because the sun comes into view as the earth spins on its axis. Whether or not God created the earth and the sun and sent one spinning in an orbit around the other isn't very relevant to a perspective that describes the sunrise in terms that come from scientific observation instead of divine revelation. We know that the sun rises because of events that occurred billions of years ago, not because of anything that God is doing today.

Because of this, even religious people find it hard not be drawn into what's called a *deistic* view of the universe, the belief that the universe was created by God at the dawn of time, wound up like a clock, and then left to run on its own with little or no further involvement by God. We don't see God as an active force intimately involved in the second-by-second operation of the universe, necessary to its very functioning. Instead, we have demoted God to the role of creator emeritus. As much as we want to believe that our prayers can somehow change the course of events, we reluctantly accept that any divine intervention would be so extraordinary that it would be very much unexpected. And so we usually find ourselves reduced to using the term *miraculous* for events that are everyday occurrences, like the birth of a child or the flight of a bumblebee.

The crisis of faith that is shaking the modern world is not so much a failure of spirituality than it is a growing awareness that the picture of God that we were raised with no longer makes sense in a world that we see through filters colored by science. These filters keep us from seeing anything that we might have otherwise thought to be supernatural or even the ordinary result of God's action. Instead, they let us see only the explanations that fit the scientific worldview, and so we no longer really expect God to disturb our everyday lives.

Even if we don't reach the point where we deny or even just doubt the existence of God, we at least end up leading our lives pretty much the same way that agnostics do. Our faith in God has become both shallow and hollow, so that our belief in God no longer shapes our attitudes or actions except in special circumstances. When we pray, we don't really expect our prayers to make any real difference, or maybe even worse, we learn to water down our prayers to make sure that we won't be disappointed when God seems to ignore our expressed desires. Instead of praying for a change in our circumstances, we pray for the ability to accept them. We move through life thinking that nothing we do makes any difference to God, that nothing we do might affect how God deals with us or the world around us. Our belief in God has become not much more than a matter of intellectual assent instead of something that actually shapes how we behave or what we expect.

This declining power of religion has been noticed by certain elements that have a vested interest in how we may or may not be controlled by religion. The result is a rising tide of religious fundamentalism that tries to reverse this trend by attacking its root, the scientific worldview itself. Believers who are swept up by this fundamentalist tide are required to accept revelation from narrowly authorized sources as the only source of truth. Ultimately, fundamentalism's limitations restrict its ability to spread its influence throughout the general population. More importantly, fundamentalism is regressive by its very nature, and the powerfully progressive forces at work in the scientific worldview remain overwhelmingly persuasive as science continues to improve its ability to make our lives longer and more comfortable, and to explain the universe around us.

Mainstream religion, then, finds itself caught between two irreconcilable forces: religious fundamentalism and scientific fundamentalism. It must find some way to integrate the spiritual zeal of religious fundamentalism with the progressive influence of science. As a crucial part of this process, mainstream religion must avoid the trap of allowing either set of fundamentalists to control the religious agenda. The recent fixation on Darwinian evolution and, by extension, the paleontology and geology that contradict the so-called young earth theories of creationism doesn't confront the more basic challenge that physics poses to religious belief. Evolution is really just a side show, a mere byproduct of the way that physics has pushed God's role in the universe to the margins of our lives and of our minds. It's not biology or geology, but physics that has forced God off of the stage. As a result, we must be able to reconcile our belief in God with physics more than with any other area of science.

# PART II: THE OLD AND THE NEW PHYSICS

## Classical Physics

In Part I, we looked at how the scientific worldview has led to a decline of religion in the modern world. While we can blame this decline on the scientific view of the world in general, it's classical physics that has had the greatest impact on religion. As we noted at the end of the last chapter, the conflict between science and religion has usually focused on biological evolution, but that's only because evolution is the most obvious way that science challenges our idea of who we are in the world. Physics, though, is the "mother of all science." That is, all of the other scientific specialties can be understood as higher-level abstractions of physics. For example, biology is a higher-level abstraction of chemistry, since biological life is really just a very complex chemical process. Chemistry, in turn, is a higher-level abstraction of physics because chemistry is all about the way that atoms interact and combine, and atoms are made up of energetic particles, the stuff that physics studies. In other words, every scientific discipline can trace its roots to the study of physics. That's why physics presents the greatest challenge to religion because it claims to describe how the universe is put together and works at its most basic level.

In fact, the first major conflict between science and religion took place in the realm of astrophysics, when Copernicus revealed that the earth moves around the sun, rather than being fixed as stated by the Bible (Psalm 93:1, for example). The Catholic Church's shocked response to this discovery was not so much because it removed people from the center of the universe and more because the Church realized that it was the first step in the development of a model of the universe that didn't require God's ongoing involvement to keep it running. Even worse, this discovery didn't depend on revelation and tradition to explain how the universe works. This new scientific approach to physical science could ignore these Church-sanctioned sources and rely instead on observation, reason, and mathematics to discover truth. The Church simply could not allow truths other than the truth that it controlled.

The fact that the way that the parts of the solar system moved could be reduced to a mathematical model meant that God could be removed from the picture altogether, and this implied that what applies to the largest objects in the universe also holds for the smallest objects as well. With enough data, theoretically the physicist could predict into the distant future all events that the data covers. Not only is God unnecessary, God is even an unwelcome intrusion whose only effect would be to blur the data. As mathematical models become a more powerful way to describe the universe, God changes from being the ongoing cause of everything that happens to being an occasional meddler. Eventually, as the Enlightenment took hold, God would become just a clockmaker who created and wound up the universe and then stepped back to watch it run down on its own. God's significance no longer required the present tense to express it.

# The Dawn of Classical Physics: Isaac Newton

Even though the use of mathematics to describe reality was revolutionary in its time, the model produced by early physicists is now a familiar one. As soon as we learned to see past the illusion of the sun rising from the horizon to being able to comprehend that the earth rotates to bring the sun into view, we found that the description of the forces of nature developed by the early physicists fit pretty well with our everyday experience. When we look at the world around us, we see it with eyes given us by Sir Isaac Newton.

You really can't overstate how important Newton is to Western thought. Not only does he stand as one of the first true scientists, but his ideas and methods have become so ingrained in our culture that it is impossible to imagine modern life without his influence everywhere. Because of the way his discoveries have shaped how we all view the world around us, even people who have never studied physics see the balls crashing around on a pool table differently than they would have, say, four hundred years ago. When we watch the actions and (equal and opposite) reactions of the balls moving about colliding with each other on the table, we see them behaving as Newton wanted us to see them. We do not see them as willful beings moving according to their own whim, but as lifeless objects that cannot help but behave according to the universal laws that govern everything from the tiniest atom to the largest galaxies. We might not be able to reproduce the math or put the principles into words, but we understand that the forces at work in the world are inflexible and inescapable. More to the point, we see that we ourselves are just as subject to those forces as those pool balls are.

Newton was born in the county of Lincolnshire, England, in 1643, three months after his father had died. After starting his education at a local village school, Newton was sent to The King's School at Grantham. After graduating in 1661, Newton was admitted to Trinity College of Cambridge University. Although the curriculum there was based on the writings of the Greek philosopher Aristotle, Newton took it upon himself to broaden his education by reading such modern philosophers and mathematician-scientists as René Descartes, Galileo, Nicolaus Copernicus, and Johannes Kepler. By the time he had received his degree in 1665, he had begun working on the mathematical theory that would evolve into his version of calculus, as well as on studies in optics and gravitation.

In 1669, Newton was chosen to fill the Lucasian Chair of Mathematics at Cambridge, the chair that Stephen Hawking currently occupies. In that position he lectured on optics for the next three years. Although he argued that light is made up of particles, he had to resort to a wave theory to account for the way light separates (diffracts) into different colors as it passes through an object, such as a prism. (While the wave theory came to be the dominant theory for the next 200 years, twentieth-century physicists, including Albert Einstein, would reintroduce and develop the particle theory, leading to the development of quantum mechanics.)

By 1679, Newton had resumed his work on mechanics, that is, the motion of bodies, focusing on gravity and how it governs the motion of planets in their orbits. This led to a more generalized study of mechanics that resulted in the publication in 1687 of the *Philosophiae Naturalis Principia Mathematica* (*A Natural Philosophy of Mathematical Principles*, also known simply as the *Principia*). It is this work that, perhaps more than any other scientific publication, revolutionized human thought about the world and our place in it.

The *Principia* presents Newton's monumental three universal laws of motion and the law of universal gravitation. Even though these laws have had to be reinterpreted in light of Einstein's theories of relativity and quantum mechanics, they still stand as a useful way to describe how things behave. When an engineer at Boeing calculates the flight characteristics of a new airplane, the engineer uses mathematical formulas substantially the same as those that Newton used to prove his laws.

## Newton's Laws and the Beginnings of Modern Science

Even though Einstein's $E=mc^2$ is the best known equation of physics, it is Newton's mathematics that has the greatest influence on our daily lives. Of course, we are all familiar with Newton's law of universal gravity, which states that things attract each other with a force that is relative to their mass (the amount of material they contain). And so, because the mass of the earth is constant, you can calculate how much mass something contains by measuring its weight (Latin *gravitas*), which is the commonplace way of describing the force of attraction between something and the earth.

Most of us aren't as familiar with Newton's mechanical laws, probably because they don't have a falling apple to capture our imaginations. Even so, they still manage to shape how we look at the world around us. Indeed, I'm sure as I list and describe them, they'll mostly seem so obvious that you will wonder what all the fuss is about.

Newton's first law of motion is also known as the *law of inertia*, which says that an object at rest stays at rest and an object in motion stays in motion, until it is acted upon by some external force. If you've ever tried to move a piano, you've no doubt understood the first part of the law: Our everyday experience tells us that things resist being moved. (Ironically, though, we know enough about gravity to assume that weight is the reason something resists being moved. In fact, it's the thing's mass that causes this resistance, so that even in weightless conditions in space, an object requires force to move it. The more mass the object has, the more force is needed.) The second part is not nearly as intuitive, however, because we rarely get the chance to watch something move when it's not also being affected by gravity and friction. For example, when we throw a ball, we see that it travels along a curved path until it hits the ground and then rolls to a stop. What might not be apparent is why the ball's path forms a curve. That's because even though it's trying to follow the law of inertia (trying to follow an infinitely long, straight path), the earth's gravity is trying to pull it straight down. As the ball moves forward, it is being pulled down at the same time, resulting in a curved path. How flat the curve is depends on the speed of the object. If it's slow, the curve is really steep, but if it's fast, the curve is nearly flat. That's why a bullet travels farther than a thrown baseball which, in turn, travels farther than a baseball that is simply dropped (without any forward motion). When it does hit the ground and begins rolling, it eventually stops because of the friction that it encounters in the air and the surface it's rolling on. Even so, anyone who has been *hit* by a thrown ball is very aware of how much that ball tends stays in motion until it meets an external force, in this case the resistance of the body that the ball hits. Ouch.

Newton's second law of motion, also known as the *law of acceleration*, is a little harder to explain and has to do with how things speed up. How fast something accelerates depends on two factors: the mass of the object and how much force is used to move the object. Of the three laws, this is the one that is perhaps most obvious to us. Every day, we experience how applying a greater amount of force to something makes it move faster. For example, to make a car go faster, we know we have to make the car's engine work harder (apply more force), and as soon as we let off on the gas, the car's speed levels off. Of course, simply because our everyday experience confirms it doesn't mean that it's obvious *why* it happens, especially when you consider the impressive mathematical proof that Newton developed to establish it as a law and not just an assumption.

Newton's third law, the *law of reciprocity*, is well known but the least understood: For every action there is an equal and opposite reaction. This is the law that makes rockets work, even in space. Our instincts tell us that rockets move because they are pushing against something, first the ground (when launched) and then the air. But then, we ask, how would a rocket work in the vacuum in space? Newton's answer is that it's not the pushing against something that makes a rocket move, but the fact that by burning fuel and expelling hot gas in one direction, the rocket is moved by an equal reaction in the opposite direction. As with the second law, force and mass pay crucial roles. The effect of the reaction depends on the amounts of mass and force involved. To illustrate, imagine two ice skaters (the ice reduces the effect of friction), one pushing against the other. Both skaters will move, and as expected, the "pushee" will move in the direction of the push, but the pusher will also move in the opposite direction. How much each skater accelerates depends on which one is heavier and by how much, so if one skater is a lot heavier, that skater will accelerate less than the lighter skater. That's why, contrary to what we see in most action movies, someone who is hit by a bullet isn't knocked backwards, because the bullet doesn't have enough mass to move the person's whole body (much). Besides, as this law shows, the person holding the gun would also be knocked backwards because, say it with me, "For every action there's an equal and opposite reaction."

As impressive as these laws were in their day and as important as they are today as a way of describing how things work, their significance goes way beyond how they're used in engineering and such. Newton's laws represented a revolution in the way we looked at the world. For the first time, we had laws which, taken together, could explain the motion of *everything*, motion that did not depend on the intervention of anything (or anyone) that was not specifically accounted for in those laws. In other words, Newton developed a set of principles that prove that, from its very beginning, the universe does not depend on God to work. In fact, one might say that because the laws account for *all* motion, it's actually impossible for God to affect that motion. Yikes. The cascading effects of these discoveries would soon undermine the religious faith that even Newton held to so fiercely.

## Newton's Laws and the Decline of Religion

Anyone who gives it much thought can't avoid realizing that Newton's laws mean that the universe is, in essence, a self-contained machine. Maybe it's one that was set in motion at the beginning by some divine First Cause, but it's also a machine that does not depend on any further involvement by that First Cause to keep it running. Even if God developed the natural laws that govern his creation, the laws themselves are self-enforcing and self-sufficient. As far as how the universe works, once God finished creating the world, he might as well have moved on to other concerns. No wonder the German philosopher Friedrich Nietzsche concluded that "God is dead." When taken to their logical conclusions, Newton's laws showed that, even if God is not "dead," it doesn't really matter to the universe, and maybe even to us.

Newton recognized that this was a ramification of his discoveries, but he didn't welcome it. As a member of the Cambridge faculty he would ordinarily be required to be an ordained clergyman in the Church of England. Although he asked for and received an exemption from that requirement, he was still a religious man. He said that he studied the Bible daily (more than he studied science, he said), and he insisted that the laws that governed the universe were designed by a Creator who continues in his role as Supreme Ruler.

In Newton's day, the established Church considered his discoveries useful for supporting the Christian faith, not undermining it. Theologians who sought to understand God through reason believed that Newton's laws supported the idea of a majestic Creative Intelligence whose grandeur was reflected in the astonishing order of the creation. While it was no longer possible for us to think of God as the animating soul of the universe, at least we could still see God as its supreme architect and (perhaps absentee) Lord.

Even though this accommodation between the Church and Newton's mechanics might have initially helped spread Newton's influence over European thinking, this harmony would be short lived. Philosophers soon realized that this mechanical picture of the universe pretty much ruled out any ongoing involvement by God because God's intervention would have to mean that there is some flaw in creation that requires God to tinker with it. And if God's creation is imperfect, then that would have to mean that God himself is imperfect, since something that is perfect cannot produce something that isn't perfect. The Church had inherited a belief in a perfect God from Greek philosophy (when Jesus called God perfect, he meant it in a moral sense), so this was an idea that the Church could not accept. This forced the Church into a logical dilemma: Either deny the truth of Newton's laws, or downplay God's role in the present-day world. In other words, the Church would have to turn its back on reason (as expressed in the mathematical proofs behind Newton's laws) or accept that God's ongoing involvement with his creation is so limited as to be practically meaningless.

The fact that Christians still haven't resolved this dilemma has contributed to the fading of religious faith that has resulted from our adopting the Newtonian view of the world. Instead of confronting it head on, we have chosen either to ignore it or to deal with it by attacking it at the fringes, as in the debates over evolution and cosmology. Ironically, though, these assaults usually take place according to the rules of the Newtonian worldview itself, because some believers try to use science to disprove its peripheral theories that they think contradicts revealed truth. Unfortunately for them, though, they end up misapplying those laws, so they end up arguing, in effect, that 2+1 can't equal 3 because 1+2 equals 3.

## Einstein's Theory of Relativity

By the end of the nineteenth century, scientists thought they had pretty much all the tools they would need to be able to write a complete history of the universe, both all the way to its beginning and into the future. Well, there were a few nagging inconsistencies, but scientists were sure that those inconsistencies would soon be eliminated and that physicists would find their path unobstructed as they moved to take their rightful place as the logical masters of the universe. Then along came Albert Einstein.

Like the other physicists before him, Einstein used mathematics to explore the remaining problems of physics, especially questions about the nature of light. Since Galileo, physicists thought of light as being made up of waves. Experiments showed that it did, indeed, act like a wave. Einstein, however, saw that light can also be thought of as being made of discrete particles (the photons of *Star Trek*'s photon torpedoes). He mathematically predicted how those particles would behave when they were put through different experiments, and as it turns out, when those experiments were actually carried out by others, they have almost always demonstrated the correctness of Einstein's calculations. When Einstein studied the implications of those calculations, he developed two theories that would rock the scientific world and provide the first credible challenge to the classical physical view of the universe pioneered by Isaac Newton. He called these theories the special and general theories of relativity.

Einstein formulated his special theory of relativity first, more than a century ago. Even as a teenager, Einstein was consumed by questions about the nature of the universe. He studied the equations of James Clerk Maxwell which described the electromagnetic force from which come electricity, light, radio, and magnetism. He wondered what it would be like to be travelling next to a beam of light, at the speed of light. We would naturally assume that the light would appear to be standing still next to the traveler, just as two cars traveling the same direction and speed on a freeway appear to each other to be standing still. The problem was, though, that Maxwell's equations didn't permit such "stationary light." Rather, Maxwell's equations worked only if light *always* traveled at the same speed (about 670 million miles per hour, by the way) relative to the observer, no matter what speed and direction the observer was moving. Or to look at it another way, if you were moving at half the speed of light (335 million MPH), and someone pointed a laser beam in the same direction, the light would still appear to you to be moving beside you at normal light speed (670 million MPH), not at one-half its "usual" speed as you would normally expect. Later, as an adult, Einstein came upon a brilliant but disturbing solution to the problem: Light always moves at a constant speed through space because, while the dimensions of space and time are relative to each other (the faster you go, the farther you go in less time), the totality of space and time are not. Instead, space and time combine to form a single, absolute entity in which all things move and have their being. Instead of being relative to time, space, and observers, the speed of light is a constant (the $c$ in $E=mc^2$) that is the boundary, if you will, of the totality and unity of space and time (space-time). Consequently, something can (theoretically) be accelerated to the speed of light, but no faster. (Sorry, *Star Trek* fans.) This is what Einstein called his special theory of relativity.

A few years later, Einstein came up with his general theory of relativity. Einstein was bothered by gravity, specifically the speed at which gravity can influence things far away. Newton's theory of gravity assumes that the gravity produced by one thing affects everything else instantly, no matter how far away they are. (The force of gravity gets weaker the farther apart things are, but the force itself is instantaneous.) According to Newton, if the sun were somehow to instantly and completely disappear (which is impossible, of course, but bear with me), then the planets would be instantly freed of the grip of the sun's gravity even before the last of the sun's light reached the earth. But according to Einstein, nothing can go faster than the speed of light, so it would seem impossible for gravity to affect objects instantaneously regardless of how far apart they are. Clearly, something had to give.

As Einstein pondered gravity, he realized that there's no difference between the effects of acceleration and the effects of gravity. We experience this when we are in a vehicle that's accelerating quickly, like an airplane on takeoff: When the plane gathers speed, its passengers are pressed against their seats in the same way that gravity would be pulling against them if the airplane was just tilted upward without speeding up. In fact, flight simulators that are used to train pilots take advantage of this by tilting backwards and forwards and side to side, giving the sensation of acceleration in different directions.

If gravity is acceleration, that raises the question, what causes this acceleration? The answer is that everything that has mass (from the tiniest subatomic particle to the largest galaxy) warps the fabric of space-time. The more mass, the greater the warping. When another object approaches this warping, it "slides down" the warped "surface" of space-time, going faster as it gets closer to the thing that's producing the gravity. Because space is warped into time, that eliminates the problem of gravity "travelling" faster than the speed of light because the warping of space-time extends everywhere all at once.

## The Special Theory and the Four-Dimensional Universe

One of the most revolutionary insights of special relativity is that space and time are really aspects of the same reality, "space-time." This has a profound effect on our understanding of how reality is constructed.

According to Einstein, time is not a river relentlessly flowing through a fixed, absolute three-dimensional space. Instead, time is another dimension alongside the three familiar dimensions of space. (People talk about time as the fourth dimension, but I don't think they really understand what this actually means.) Traveling through the dimension of time is like traveling through the other three dimensions of space-time. More to the point, though, is the fact that traveling along one of any of the four dimensions affects how fast you travel along the other three dimensions.

To understand this, let's consider an orca whale on the water. Assuming that it is heading straight north at its maximum speed, its speed along the east-west axis is zero because it doesn't move further east or west, just north, right? Now imagine that the whale turns and heads straight east; all of its speed is along the east-west axis and its speed along the north-south axis is zero. But if the whale is traveling due northeast at the same speed, then less of its speed is northward and less of its speed is eastward. (I won't bore you with the actual math. Trust me; it's a lot easier for both of us, and the whale wouldn't understand it anyway.) Finally, it dives and heads down at a 45-degree angle at the same speed. Then even less of its speed is northward, even less of its speed is eastward, and more of its speed is downward.

Just as travel through the three dimensions of space means that travel through one dimension necessarily reduces the speed of travel through the other two dimensions, this also applies to the fourth dimension of time. In other words, the faster you travel through space, the slower you move through time. Or another way of looking at it, the faster you travel, time itself "slows down." (Believe it or not, this has been verified experimentally by synchronizing two extremely precise clocks and then flying one in a plane at a very high rate of speed. The two clocks were then compared, and the one on the plane was found to be a few ticks slower than the one that didn't fly.)

The logical consequence of this is that time and space exist simultaneously; just as you can move freely in any direction in the three dimensions of space, so you can (theoretically) move freely in any direction in the four dimensions of space-time. (The fact that you can't really go back in time is a conundrum, however, that is beyond the scope of this book.) The past, the future, and the now exist simultaneously. This perspective makes it easier to see how God could transcend time, because time is not a river sweeping God along, but instead, the universe is a closed system of space-time that exists within the mind of God, as it were.

## Special Relativity and the Subjective Universe

The aspect of Einstein's theories that we find easiest to understand is his description of the relativity of motion. We all have had the experience of sitting in a moving car watching the road zoom by at 60 miles an hour, only to have our gaze interrupted by a car overtaking us at (what appears to be) five miles an hour. We intuitively understand that the car appears to be moving at five miles an hour because it's traveling five miles per hour faster than the car we're in, even though both are traveling 60 to 65 miles per hour along the road. This relative difference in speed is not just an illusion, however. If instead of overtaking us, the other car were to come up from behind and collide with us, the initial collision would be relatively minor and, assuming both drivers managed to keep control of their cars, would result in little damage or injury. (We'd still be able to sue the other driver for whiplash, though.) This is true, even though both cars were hurtling through space at 60 and 65 miles per hour, *plus* whatever additional speed they gain from the earth's rotation and orbit around the sun, and so on.

Einstein's special theory takes this intuitive relativity to its ultimate conclusion, however. While we understand the relativity of motion, we view all motion as relative within an absolute, fixed space. In other words, we think of a point in space as being the center from which the three dimensions of space spread out and relative to which all things in the universe are located and moving. Einstein, however, discovered that *all* things are relative, not to a point in space, but to the speed of light. As we've seen, this ties into the idea of the four-dimensional universe, of course: The faster you move through space, the slower you move through time, and vice versa.

This means that there is no fixed, absolute, objective point from which the motion of all objects can be measured, no "home" point that we can use to find where we are in space-time. Instead, everything is relative to all other things (again, limited by the speed of light). So, in a sense, the entire universe is subjective, not objective, and all things can be comprehended only as they relate the to the one doing the comprehending. Yes, that means that you really are the center of the universe. Try not to make too much of that, though, because I'm the center of the universe, too.

## *E=mc²* and the Energetic Universe

Just about everyone is familiar with Einstein's summary equation for his special theory of relativity, $E=mc^2$, and most understand that it has something to do with converting matter to energy. Of course, it explains how an atomic bomb works by splitting or combining atoms (depending on the type of bomb) to "destroy" them and release their energy, mainly as heat. If you unpack the equation, you can easily see how a small amount of matter can produce so much destructive energy. The $E$ stands for the amount of energy that is released, while the $m$ stands for the mass of the matter that is the input for the equation. The $c$ is the constant, which is conventionally described as "the speed of light." Of course, as we've seen, the speed of light is best thought of as the ultimate limit, the "that which you can't go beyond." This constant limits the size of the universe, for example, because the universe cannot expand faster than the speed of light. So the amount of energy contained in a bit of matter is the amount (mass) of the matter multiplied by the *square* of the upper limit of the universe, as it were. That's why a bomb ironically named Little Boy could destroy practically the entire city of Hiroshima (and, tragically, those who lived there), in spite of the fact that it was not very efficient and ended up spreading most of its uranium over the surrounding landscape.

The underlying meaning of the equation, however, is not that you can convert a small amount of matter into an incredible amount of energy, but that matter *is* energy, just in a "congealed" form. The atoms that we picture as being little solar systems made up of very tiny solid particles of material stuff are actually made up of chunks of energy that happen to behave like particles (which we'll look at more closely later). That means that the universe is not made up of static matter, but instead, that all things are made up of energy.

That should have a profound impact on how we look at the world around us. For one thing, it means that the distinction we make between matter and energy, between the solid, liquid, and gaseous stuff we usually think of as being the most real, and the light, heat, and electrical energy we tend to think of as transitory, that distinction is an illusion. If we connect energy with spirit (both being forces that are thought to animate the material world), then that means that the universe is fundamentally spiritual. We'll look closer at this idea when we explore the implications of quantum theory.

## The General Theory and the Warped Universe

Einstein's special theory forced us to rethink our experience of time and space, to see that motion in space and the passage of time are essentially the same. His general theory of relativity presents an even greater challenge to how we understand the form of space-time itself. According to intuition and our high-school geometry teachers, space consists of three dimensions that extend straight out from some central point. (The exact location of that point is disputed by numerous Chambers of Commerce.) On the other hand, Einstein's general theory of relativity describes space in a very different way. According to that theory, the presence of mass causes space to be curved into the dimension of time in such a way that something traveling along that curve is continually accelerated. That, in a nutshell, is how gravity works.

For the first time, physics was presenting a description of reality that is wildly at odds with how our minds insist on perceiving it. According to Einstein's theory, the fundamental nature of space-time is so different from our actual experience that it is impossible for us to picture it in our minds. Our brains are so "hardwired" to think in terms only of three spatial dimensions that we can't really picture how gravity works. The closest we can come is to represent it by using a two-dimensional plane that appears to warp in three dimensions (think of a bowling ball on a trampoline), showing how the warping of three-dimensional space extends into the fourth dimension of time. But this is no more than a rough approximation that only suggests how gravity becomes acceleration, instead of the constant "pull" that we experience. This means that the fundamental nature of space-time is not just hidden from us; it is actually structured in a way that it is impossible for us to envision.

As we look closer at the way that fundamental reality is portrayed by the new physics, we discover that we have to abandon our commonsense experience, to accept the truth of this portrayal even when we can only understand it through logic, not through our experience or mental imagery. We might be tempted to liken this acceptance to faith, but it is not a blind acceptance of what we can't prove. Instead, it is an acknowledgement of what we *can* prove even when it is hard to accept.

## Quantum Theory

Classical physics deals with how matter and energy behave pretty much at the everyday level. That is, it has traditionally dealt with the material world largely as we see it around us. Even when it deals with the motion of planets, stars, and galaxies, it does so in a way that fits with what we observe in our own surroundings. No doubt that is why the findings—and implications—of classical physics have become so ingrained into our culture and thinking.

Einstein's theories are most meaningful when dealing with things at the extremes of mass and acceleration, however, so they are much more difficult for us to appreciate with our intuition. While classical physics is able to evoke an "of course!" reaction in us, Einstein's theories of relativity force us to think of reality in a way that defies common sense. As we go faster, time slows down. The presence of mass warps space into time, and the more mass something has, the more extreme the warping is. As other things approach this warped space, they begin to accelerate toward the thing that is causing space to warp and (this is the truly weird part) they continue to accelerate "toward" the thing even when they are firmly in contact with it.

About the same time that Einstein was developing his theories, though, another group of physicists were, like him, looking at the question, What if light is made up of particles (or more precisely, packets of energy) instead of the waves described by classical physics? Like Einstein, they concluded that any difference between matter and energy is simply a difference in state, not in kind, sort of like the difference between water and ice. And as Einstein did, they used a rigorous mathematical analysis to study the nature of matter and energy, but they came up with results that so wildly contradicted our intuitive grasp of reality that even Einstein had trouble accepting them. Indeed, the implications of quantum mechanical theory (named for the quantum, or energy packet, that is its subject) are so scandalous that scientists surely would have abandoned it long ago except for the fact that it has been spectacularly successful at predicting the outcomes of experiments. And these outcomes are so unexpected that they seem to defy reason itself. In other words, much to everyone's amazement, experimental results have confirmed even the most unintuitive aspects of quantum mechanics. The following chapters describe some of the more scandalous aspects of quantum theory and how they change how we view the universe and God's place in it.

## Quantum Theory and the Ambiguous Universe

As with Einstein's relativity theories, quantum mechanics began with the question, "What if light is composed of particles instead of waves?" It turns out, though, that the "instead of" is misleading because light behaves like a wave *and* like a particle. You'll note that I was careful not to say "like waves and particles," because I didn't want to be misleading: Light is not made up of waves of particles (like the waves on the sea are made up of water molecules, for example). No, the wave nature of light and the particle nature of light are mutually exclusive. That is, light is made up of waves-that-are-not-particles, and light is also made up of particles-that-are-not-waves.

One of the classic experiments used to test quantum theory illustrates this. It's the so-called double-slit experiment. To perform the experiment, you take a device that can fire a single particle of light (called a photon) and a device that can detect a single photon. (I know, that begs the question by assuming that light is made up of particles, but we'll deal with that later.) Place the photon shooter on one side of an opaque screen that has two slits in it and two photon detectors on the other side of the screen, each behind one of the slits. Make the photon shooter fire photons at the screen, and note that each photon detector registers each photon that manages to pass through one of the slits, pretty much as you'd expect.

Now replace the photon shooter with a regular source of light (a light bulb) and replace the photon detectors with conventional photographic film. Turn on the light bulb so that the film is exposed to the light. Develop the film and examine the results. If the experiment was set up properly, what you'll see is two dark patches (this being a negative image, after all) where the slits were. But between and around them, you'll see a strange pattern of light and dark areas. This is what's called an interference pattern, which is what happens when two sets of waves collide. (Try dropping two stones into a still pond. When the resulting waves collide, they will produce an interference pattern.) Thus proving that light is made up of waves.

Now comes the weird part: Put a new film behind the screen. Replace the light bulb with the photon shooter. Now shoot a whole lot of photons one at a time at the screen, until the film is sufficiently exposed. Now, a photon, being a particle, can only do one of three things: It can hit the screen where a slit isn't (it will either bounce off or be absorbed and converted to heat, depending on how reflective the screen is), it can pass through one slit, or it can pass through the other slit. So when you develop the film, you'd expect to see two dark bars where the slits were, and nothing else, right?

Wrong. What you'll see is the same results you got when the light bulb was (presumably) sending out waves of light. But stop and think for a minute. The photons were fired one at a time. There was nothing for any of them to interfere with or be interfered with. Each just passed from the photon shooter through the slit to the film all by itself. And yet, somehow, each "knew" it should behave as though it were a wave that was interfered with by a wave passing through the other slit.

If you think that's weird, wait until you find out what happens when you put a photon detector back into the experiment. That'll come in a later chapter, though.

So light is made up of both waves and particles. But remember what we learned from Einstein's $E=mc^2$: Matter is energy and energy is matter. The only difference between the two is the extent to which the particles of energy (quanta) are held together to form atoms.

Those of us who have had a basic science education tend to picture atoms as consisting of bundles of round protons and neutrons (that look a lot like Styrofoam balls painted red and yellow, usually) surrounded by little black balls swirling around the nucleus of the atom in their little orbits. So the atom is actually just a very, *very* tiny structure made up of particles that are the "real" matter.

Well, that isn't quite right. For one thing, the atom isn't anywhere near as compact as the usual model would have it. Imagine that you are standing in the center of domed football arena. A fly lands on your hand. If the arena were the size of an atom, the fly would be about the size of the atom's nucleus. More important-ly, though, is the realization that these things that we think of as particles are also dimensionless waves. So rather than being made up of tiny little "solid" particles, matter—what seems most real and substantial to us—is really just made up of trillions and trillions of wavelike bits (or bitlike waves, if you prefer) of energy. So not only is the solidity, the substantiality of matter apparent-ly an illusion, the very foundation of reality is ambigu-ous. We and our world are made up of particles or waves, or maybe both, or maybe neither.

## Quantum Theory and the Uncertain Universe

Werner Heisenberg was one of the most important researchers in the field of quantum mechanics. In 1932, at the age of 30 he received the Nobel Prize in physics for his work. (At 30 I was still trying to figure out what I wanted to be when I grew up.) He is probably best known for his "uncertainty principle," which in its sim-plest form, says that it is possible to know a particle's position or to know its momentum (direction and speed), but not both. In other words, the more you know about the position of the particle, the less certainty you can have about its momentum, and vice versa. It's kind of like looking at a distant car ferry on the Puget Sound. Because both ends of the ferry are identical, you can't tell which direction it's traveling unless you watch it over time to see which way it's going. And once you've fig-ured out its direction and speed, it's no longer where it was, so you've lost your ability to be sure of exactly where it is at any given moment.

As we've seen before, classical physics gives us a view of the world that's strongly deterministic. A deterministic worldview says that each event is produced by a specific set of conditions that, if they could be reproduced exactly, would cause the same event to occur again. If you know the initial state of a system with absolute precision, then you could predict how that system will behave all the way to eternity. A game of pool is an example. According to classical mechanics, if you know the exact position of the ten balls after they've been racked, the exact position of the cue ball, the exact position, angle and force applied to the cue stick when it strikes the cue ball, then you will know how hard and where the cue ball will strike the other balls, and consequently how hard and where they will strike each other, and so on. Assuming you knew everything you needed to know with complete accuracy, you would know the exact location of each ball when it finally came to rest.

According to Heisenberg's uncertainty principle, though, this "thought experiment" is based on a false assumption. It is *not* possible to know with absolute precision the angle and the force of the cue stick as it sets the game in motion. This is not, as you might think, simply the result of imprecise measurement. Instead, it is a mathematically inherent property of the very act of measurement itself. (Now, having said this, I should in all honesty point out that Heisenberg was dealing with extremely small quantities of measurement, on subatomic scales. The principle becomes less and less significant—but doesn't disappear altogether—as the scales increase.) As a result, the purely theoretical idea that the future can be predicted based on present conditions does not hold water. Or to put it another way, the universe isn't strictly deterministic after all. Instead of being able to predict a specific event (or, more precisely, a given quantity) based on current conditions, the best we can do is to calculate the *probability* that a given event will occur. The possible events are distributed along a probability curve (often in the shape of the dreaded bell curve we were graded against in school). It is only when the event occurs (that is, the quantity is measured) that the curve "collapses" into the single value that is measured. We'll get back to this in more detail in the next chapter.

By now you should be throwing up your hands and exclaiming, "But wait! Doesn't this undermine the very foundations of the scientific process, which is the ability to predict future events based on precise knowledge of present conditions?" (See how smart you are?) Indeed it does, and that's why the implications of quantum theory were thought to be so disturbing that at the beginning of the twentieth century. nearly every scientist who wasn't a quantum theorist felt compelled to challenge them.

Of course, we can't simply dismiss the traditional scientific worldview because it doesn't fit the uncertainty principle. This is, after all, a crack in the foundation, not an utter demolition of the entire building. Even so, the uncertainty principle does stand as a challenge to the scientific fundamentalists who claim that science has the potential to provide complete and accurate answers to all possible questions. At the very least, scientists should be humble enough to recognize that, beyond death and taxes, nothing in life is certain, not even science.

## Quantum Theory and the Probabilistic Universe

We need to take a closer look at this idea of a probability wave because its implications are so staggering that even Einstein could only dismiss it with his famous statement that is usually paraphrased as "God does not play dice with the universe." As we noted in the previous chapter, the classical view of the processes that drive everything in the universe is that they are deterministic, that is, that everything has a specific cause, and every cause has a specific effect. Sure, multiple causes can combine to produce a different effect than would be produced by any single cause, but in theory at least, if you know enough about all of the causes, you can with certainty predict the effect. Further, if you know enough about the effect, you can determine with certainty its cause(s). According to this view, there is no real randomness, no element of chance, and so there's no freedom in even the loosest sense of the term. Everything that exists, human beings included, is tied to its past and to its inescapable destiny. Even our free will is just an illusion, a byproduct of psychological processes that trick the brain into thinking that somehow it is choosing freely when in fact it is merely running a program very much like the computer that it is. From this perspective, the human mind has much more in common with a silicon chip than it does with the soul of religious faith.

Of course, we can't argue with the fact that the part of the universe that we can see is highly deterministic. Otherwise, science couldn't work at all because it wouldn't be able to reach conclusions from experimentation, and it wouldn't be able to use those conclusions to predict future events. In fact, everyday life would be quite unimaginable if we couldn't rely on the process of cause and effect. But quantum mechanics has demonstrated, both mathematically and through experiment, that such reliable determinism is not true at the subatomic level, at least, and that you can only determine the probability of a particular effect.

For example, if you add enough energy to an atom, an electron in the atom will reposition itself, such as by moving from one location to another farther away from the nucleus, or sometimes by being knocked off the atom altogether. (This is how solar panels produce electricity, by the way.) Precisely when and where that electron goes can only be predicted within a range of probabilities. While it is likely that the electron will reposition itself within the atom, there is a really, really, *really* tiny chance that it could end up on the other side of the universe.

When put in a graph, the range of possibilities forms a wave or curve, somewhat like the famous bell curve. At the middle and highest point in the curve is the likeliest place where the electron will appear, while the fringes of the curve, the values so close to zero that they are infinitesimally small, are the least likely places where the electron will appear, such as the other side of the universe or even one foot away. (The same principle applies to *when* the electron will move, too.) It isn't until this probability wave collapses that the new position of the electron is actually realized, however. This is as weird as the notion that sometimes 1+1≠2, and yet experiments have demonstrated it over and over again.

So if the subatomic is completely random, how is it possible that pretty much all events in our experience are so (sometimes boringly) predictable? Look closer at that probability curve and its bell shape. Nearly all the possible ways that a given subatomic particle can behave fit within the range in the middle, which just happens to be the set of possibilities with few or no unexpected consequences. In other words, within that range are such possibilities as the electron not moving, or moving one level out, or even jumping out of the atom and into a wire that will carry its electrical charge to a battery (the solar panel, remember?). Now consider that trillions and trillions of subatomic events are occurring each second just within the book you're holding in your hands. That means that, of those trillions (and trillions) of events that are happening, just about all of them fit within that middle range of the probability curve, that range of trivial differences. To be truly noticeable, a *lot* of those trillions of random events would have to take place outside the middle range of the probability curve *and* just happen to combine in a way that you could notice. And no doubt that does happen, but with such a near-infinite rarity that it makes flipping a coin a billion times and having it come up heads every time seem ordinary.

One way to think of these millions of random events combining to produce an essentially predictable result is to consider an hourglass. It's filled with thousands, maybe millions of grains of sand. You can't say with certainty when each grain will pass through the neck of the glass and how fast it will drop (it might or might not get caught up with another grain, for example, and slow down as a result). Still, because of the effect of the averaging of the speed of all these grains, you can count on the top half of the hourglass being empty pretty darn close to the hour mark.

And so there can be no doubt: the universe is driven, not by processes that follow predictable and inflexible laws, but by a combination of truly random subatomic events that, by their sheer number and probability, just happen to add up to what appears to be laws governing the universe. So what seems to us to be strict, unbendable laws is actually the combination of the effects of random-yet-highly-probable events. Quite a different picture of the universe than that given to us by Newton, no?

## Quantum Theory and the Empirical Universe

Earlier I told you about the double-slit experiment which showed that light behaves as a particle or as a wave, but never both at the same time. The behavior depends on how you set up the experiment. If you set it up to detect photons individually, that's what you get. If you set up the experiment to detect the waves of light, then you get results that fit with that expectation. That's weird enough, but it gets even weirder when you set up the experiment to detect both waves and photons.

Imagine setting up the double-slit experiment using the single-photon shooter and the photographic film. As you may recall, even though you shoot one photon at a time, therefore (seemingly) ruling out the possibility of two waves interfering with each other, you still end up with the interference patterns you would expect if you were sending waves through the two slits. It is as though the photon, which is supposed to be a tiny particle in a single location in space, is behaving like a wave interfering with other waves. Now imagine that you set up the photon detectors such that they don't impede the photons' path through the slits and to the photographic film, but so you can detect which slit a given photon passes through.

Given this arrangement, you'd expect that the interference pattern would still appear on the film as before, right? You'd be wrong, though. As long as the photon detectors are turned on and registering the path that each photon takes, the interference pattern disappears, but if the photon detectors are turned off, the interference pattern reappears! (The actual apparatus is more complicated than this, but this gives you an idea of how it's set up and the effective results.) It's as though the photons know whether they're being observed as particles or as waves and act accordingly!

One way to interpret this is as the effect of the Heisenberg uncertainty principle: Before each photon is detected, it's uncertain whether it's wavelike or particlelike. But as soon as it's detected as a photon, that is, a particle that passes through just one slit, then the probability wave is collapsed by this observation and it "becomes" a photon, eliminating the possibility of it behaving as a wave. Remember, the detector itself doesn't interact with the photon, so it doesn't (directly, at least) affect the photon's path or behavior. The only thing that changes is whether the detector is actually used to detect the path of each photon.

This is what is so scandalous about quantum theory: It is the intention of the observer that decides the outcome of the experiment! While physicists still debate the details of how this happens, most quantum physicists admit that somehow the conscious observer plays a fundamental role in the ongoing processes of reality. This turns the notion of strong objectivity on its head: instead of having an objective existence that isn't affected by the presence of an observer, it would appear that the smallest events (that is, those that occur at the subatomic level) depend in some way on some kind of observation. In other words, not only does the tree falling in the forest *not* make a sound if there's no one there to hear it, it doesn't even fall if there's no one there to see it!

For those of us who have been trained to think in terms of material realism, this presents a problem: If consciousness is merely an epiphenomenon—a byproduct, if you will—of the biochemical processes of the brain, how could that consciousness affect external events? It can't, unless consciousness is not a mere product of the material world, but instead an underlying *cause* of the material world. To make any sense of this requires us to rethink our understanding of the nature of consciousness, God, and our very selves. And that is what this book is all about. (What, I'm halfway through the book and I'm just getting to it?!)

## Quantum Theory and the Entangled Universe

If you've ever held two pairs of polarized sunglasses, maybe you've seen how turning one pair 90 degrees to the other will almost completely block the light passing through the two of them. This is because the light that passes through one set of lenses is filtered so that the light waves allowed through are traveling only along a particular pair of axes, say $x$ and $z$, while light passing through the second set of lenses is filtered so that the only light waves allowed through are traveling only along a different pair of axes, say $y$ and $z$. The result, of course is that practically no light passes through the second lens because the first has already filtered almost out all the light waves that would be otherwise be passed by the second.

Of course, as we've already seen, light is both a wave and a particle, so another way to describe what happens is that each lens filters out photons whose polarity does not match the direction of the polarization of the lens.

Now imagine an experiment in which an apparatus can produce two photons and send them in opposite directions. This apparatus can produce the photons in such a way that they are *entangled*, that is, their polarization axes are in the same direction. You and a friend are separated, each standing in the path of one of the two photons and wearing identical polarized sunglasses. Because the two photons are entangled, you know that if you can see your photon, then your friend can likewise see her photon.

Here comes the weird part, though. Seeing the photon means that its probability wave function collapses; that is, before it was observed, it could have been in any of a number of different polarities, but observing it caused the probability function to collapse to the single state that you happened to observe. And because the other photon was entangled with yours, your friend observed her photon as having the same polarity. If, between the time that the photons were released and the time that yours reached your sunglasses, you had flipped your sunglasses 90 degrees and then saw the photon (thus collapsing its probability wave and fixing its polarity), your friend would find that she couldn't see its partner because her sunglasses were still oriented along the original polarization. Somehow your friend's photon "knew" what polarization it was to assume as a result of its partner having been observed by you, even though the two photons were far apart from each other.

Albert Einstein was so bothered by the uncertainty principle that he teamed up with two other physicists (Boris Podolsky and Nathan Rosen) to write a paper that they titled, "Can quantum mechanical description of physical reality be considered complete?" to challenge the uncertainty principle. This paper presented a thought experiment (called the EPR paradox) that was essentially the same as ours. In this paper, they concluded that, since the outcome predicted by the uncertainty principle was patently illogical, the uncertainty principle could not be true. Instead, they insisted that there has to be an objective reality which exists before a measurement takes place and that the act of measuring merely confirms the reality, it doesn't play any part in producing that reality. If there is any uncertainty, they said, it has to be due to the presence of so-called hidden local variables that determine how the two photons correlated. Only this, they insisted, would be able to account for the ability of the state of one photon in the pair to affect the state of the other, even though they were separated from each other. Otherwise, because the photons were traveling away from each other at the speed of light, somehow a signal would have to pass between them *faster* than the speed of light, which is impossible according to Einstein's special theory of relativity. Thus, the outcome predicted by the uncertainty principle would violate the principle of locality, that is, the assumption that things separated in space can affect each other only by a chain of events that connect them. (Remember my example of the TV signal passing through space between the TV station and the TV set.)

When Einstein and his colleagues formulated the EPR paradox, experimental physicists didn't have the technology available to them to perform the thought experiment in the real world. Since then, though, physicists have been able to develop several ways of reproducing the experiment, and the results have consistently supported the uncertainty principle. Sorry, Albert.

Einstein thought that the fact that the results of the experiment that the uncertainty principle proposed would require that events be nonlocal was enough to prove that the principle is untrue, or at least to undermine it. The principle of locality was so basic to the scientific worldview that it was inconceivable that it could be violated. And yet science has since established, beyond a doubt, that at the subatomic level at least, things widely separated in space can affect each other simultaneously. The universe is nonlocal, after all.

So what are we to conclude from this? If two things that are separated in space can affect each other in a way that is impossible given the limits on how fast information can travel through space, then that means that space—distance—itself is an illusion, that the spatial separation between two things (in this case, two particles) is illusory. Instead, the two things are entangled with each other in a way that makes any apparent separation between them irrelevant. In other words, everything is everywhere all at once. No wonder they call this "quantum weirdness."

## Quantum Theory and the Holographic Universe

One way to explain the quantum entanglement we encountered in the last chapter is to use the controversial paradigm of the holographic universe. Although even its strongest supporters don't consider this paradigm to be developed enough to qualify as a full-blown theory, it is still useful for helping understand this quantum weirdness. It is inspired by the nature of holographic photographs (holograms), the three-dimensional photographs that are mainly used today to discourage the counterfeiting of valuable items like credit cards and software. These common holograms are the reflective type, though, so they don't show the most interesting aspects of holography that can only be seen in the transparent kind that were the first to be developed.

Holograms are produced by splitting a light source (preferably a highly coherent light, like a laser beam) and shining half on the object being photographed and half directly on the photographic film. After it is developed, the resulting image on the film appears to be just a wave interference pattern (sound familiar?). The magic happens when you shine a light like the one used to produce the image through the film: A truly three-dimensional image of the object that was photographed appears just beyond the film. Unlike other 3D images captured on film, this isn't just a combination of two separate images that are directed to each eye, producing a simulated 3D effect. Instead, this is a true 3D image, so that moving the observer relative to the image actually "moves" the image, revealing parts of the image that were previously hidden.

A conventional photograph can only record a "slice" of the light that bounces off an object in all directions. A lens captures part of that light and then spreads it out into a cone shape. The photographic film in effect, slices through the cone to capture a flat segment of the cone. That's why a photograph can only record two dimensions (corresponding to the slice of the cone) of information.

Holographic photography works differently, however. Instead of using a lens to create a cone that can be "sliced," a holographic photograph captures all of the light bouncing off the object in the direction of the film.

Normally this would produce no real image because of the way the light is scattered when it hits the film. But the so-called reference light that shines directly on the film combines with the light from the object to produces a wave interference pattern that locks in the image of the object, or more precisely, the light bouncing off the object every which way, and not just the light passing straight from the object to a lens. Then, when you pass through the film a light source similar to the one used to capture the image, this "unlocks" the information stored in the interference wave pattern to produce an information-rich 3D image.

Another intriguing property of a transparent holo-gram is that the entire image is distributed across the entire hologram, so that if you cut off a piece of the hologram and then shine the light through it, the image displayed is not just part of the object (as you'd get with a regular photo), but the entire object, although in less detail. Thus the "whole" in hologram refers not only to its ability to record the whole object, but also the fact that the whole image is recorded by the whole photograph.

Finally, a possibly relevant characteristic of a holo-gram is the way that you can use different frequencies of light to record multiple images on the hologram, each of which can then be "released" by shining light of the matching frequency through the holographic film.

So how does this apply to the way that the universe is put together? The holographic paradigm of the uni-verse suggests to us that the universe is really a result of the interaction of all the "wavy particles" that make up the universe. That is, the atoms of the universe do not consist of discrete particles, but rather the interaction (interference) of the "wavy particles" with each other. Consequently, the universe can be understood as a hologram in which the whole is present in all parts and which is rich with information, even more information than what can be "decoded" through the usual means. An intriguing aspect of this paradigm is that it was arrived at by two different routes: through quantum theory and through brain research which found that the brain might work in a holographic manner. In the case of brain research, it's becoming more and more clear that memories are not stored as separate bits of information in a specific location in the brain, the way a computer stores its memory. Instead, the brain stores memories through the creation of interference patterns of wavelike phenomena. And so the brain stores memories holographically throughout the brain. Other brain functions (such as cognition and consciousness) also appear to be produced by wavelike phenomena. Taken together, the holographic paradigm of physics and the holographic paradigm of brain research produce some really interesting ideas about how the mind and the external world might interact in a way that is not limited by the locality of our bodies.

# PART III: GOD IN THE DETAILS

## Quantum Theology

Chances are very good that if you were to poll a hundred people and asked them to describe God in a single sentence, most of them would say something like, "God is the one who created everything."

In Western religions, at least, God is first and foremost thought of as being the creator of the universe. It's no coincidence that the first sentence of the Jewish and Christian scriptures is, "In the beginning, God created the heavens and the earth." The first statement of faith that was widely accepted among Christians, the Nicene Creed, begins, "We believe in one God, the Father Almighty, Maker of heaven and earth, and of all things visible and invisible."

If God is above all else the creator of the universe, then it is natural for us to expect to be able to learn about God's nature from his creation. From at least the days of the Psalmist, we have looked upward at the splendor of the heavens to seek the face of God, even after Copernicus sparked the revolution that changed the way we view the universe. If you've ever been able to get away from the lights of the city to view the night sky the same way people in ancient times saw it, then you can understand how this impulse is practically irresistible.

Indeed, as our picture of the universe has matured from a dome arcing from horizon to horizon (the firmament of Genesis) to an expanse with boundaries billions of light years away (which translates into a number of miles so great that there aren't even words for it), our sense of the magnificence of God has actually grown with it. However, we can be deceived by this habit of seeking God in the heavens because it tricks us into thinking of God only in big terms, a God so great and powerful that he must transcend us mere mortals and the material world which contains us. If we go further to reflect on the nature of the God who must be responsible for Newton's and, in a different way, for Einstein's universe, that God must seem even more distant from us in space, in time, and even in his very nature.

A theology that is based on the insights of quantum theory, however, describes a very different God, a God who is so close to where and who we are that it is hard to tell him apart from us. This is not just because quantum mechanics deals with extremely tiny stuff, but even more so because it describes a universe of indefinite boundaries, where the difference between me and the things around me is much more a matter of degree than of kind. In this universe, there is no border that separates the oxygen molecules in my body from the oxygen molecules in the air, and the little bits of stuff that make up the atoms in my body are not located only in the space that contains my body, but instead pervade the whole universe. Perhaps more important, the basic role of the collapse of the wave function, which is to say, the fulfillment of the potential of each moment, means that somehow a conscious being is responsible for the existence of everything that is, and since I know that *I'm* conscious, well….

This, of course, is pretty close to heresy, but it is heretical in the same way as when we changed the way we think of God to take Copernicus into account. That was regarded as heresy in *its* time. But as with all other scientific truths, we cannot ignore the truth of quantum theory simply because it's inconvenient, not unless we are willing to put faith and truth at odds with each other. And so we must, with courage and perhaps even a bit of recklessness, consider the implications that quantum theory has for our understanding of God's nature and history.

## Finding God in the Ambiguous Universe: Surrendering Our Certitude

Maybe we human beings are at our most sinful when we claim to have special knowledge of who God is, what he's like, and what his will is. That's really what idolatry is all about: Instead of submitting ourselves to an unfathomable God, we squeeze God into a container of our own making, in the process claiming that our own concerns are his. If we dread hunger, then we assume that God can also get hungry, and so we attempt to win him over by feeding him with sacrifices of food. If we long to be loved, then we assume that God must crave our praise and adoration. We create God in our own image and then claim that this image is the only one that accurately represents who God is and what God wants.

Even if we don't create a God in our image, we at least choose the image that, in our pride, we insist is the only true way to represent God. Of course, in the major monotheistic traditions (Judaism, Christianity, and Islam), we don't create graven images that we think accurately depict God, but we do paint mental pictures and descriptions that we think are definitive, even if we are willing to admit that they are not complete. Unfortunately, these descriptions usually come from the idealism of classical Greek philosophy. As a result, we characterize God as being omnipotent, omniscient, omnipresent, all the omni- qualities that push God so far away that we find ourselves unable to relate to him in any way except as an abstract idea.

In so doing, we make absolute what really must be relative, because the way God reveals himself is unavoidably partial and imperfect. Contrary to what we might think, however, the way that God reveals himself only in part is not just God being capricious. Instead, it is an essential quality of God and of the creation through which God reveals himself. As quantum mechanics shows us, the essence of nature itself is uncertain, and it defies our attempts to gain complete knowledge of what happens at the subatomic level. So, too, God's true nature must elude our attempts to know him completely.

For this reason, as we continue on, we must be able to set aside our views of who and what God is, be they orthodox or otherwise, and we must be open to seeing God from new perspectives. Furthermore, we must accept as inevitable that each perspective produces only a limited understanding and, like the particle/wave experiments, yields only the results that we were looking for, at least to a certain extent. But we must remember that, for this very reason, whatever conclusions we can reach are not only incomplete, they don't even exclude other conclusions that may seem to completely contradict ours.

While this may trouble us and tempt us to think that we can never understand God as he is, we should remember that if God is anything close to the traditional view (that is, the description of God that begins every word with *omni-*), then this incomplete understanding is unavoidable and even necessary. That's because our limitations mean that we can never comprehend God's all-knowing, all-powerful, all-present nature.

But it's not just our own limitations that restrict our ability to take in the fullness of the divine reality. If we have learned anything from the way physics has developed over the past century or so, it is that every perspective must be seen as limited by the scale it applies to: Newton's laws works best at the everyday scale of ordinary experience, Einstein's theories apply most clearly at extremes of speed and mass, and quantum theories best explain events at subatomic scales. Just as the essential nature of the universe is simultaneously different at different scales, so the essential nature of God is simultaneously different from different perspectives. Whatever we can say about God that is true at one level is likely to be untrue at another. We must never forget that whenever we begin a sentence with, "God is…" we must also be willing to consider the possibility that "God is not…" might be equally true in another context, from another viewpoint.

# Finding God in the Uncertain Universe: The Elusiveness of God

We don't really trust faith. When people want to say that they believe something so strongly that it affects how they think and live, they often resort to "fact speak": I *know* there is a God, I *know* that I'm going to heaven, I *know* that Jesus was raised from the dead. We assume that it is the things that we know that are most real, and we think that the more we know, the more trustworthy that knowledge is. Faith, on the other hand, is what is left when facts fail. Not having been there with a watch on my wrist, I cannot know for sure that the six days in which God created the heavens and the earth were not 24-hour days like our own, so I have to confess that I merely *believe* that to be the case. Faith is what we resort to when knowledge fails.

The problem with this attitude, though, is that it puts way too much weight on knowledge. It assumes that factual information is the most important, the most reliable information that we can have. Maybe this is a carryover from the classical worldview, which valued reason and the ideas that support reason as being the only trustworthy way to approach the world. In any case, it is one of the roots of the ongoing conflict between science and religion: The realm of "facts" has pretty much been surrendered to science, and when religion attempts to state something as a fact, doing so is considered to be overconfident and even out of bounds. (And yet this is ironic, considering that when science is most true to itself, it never speaks of facts but of data that supports a theory.)

When theology takes the findings of quantum mechanics seriously, it must recognize that it cannot rely on knowledge to be the basis of our approach to God or to anything else, for that matter. While we must be careful not to apply Heisenberg's uncertainty principle too broadly, at least we should respect its primary lesson that complete knowledge is impossible, that our information is by its very nature incomplete and inexact. If that is true for our knowledge of a subatomic particle, how much more true must it be when it comes to "knowing" God!

For that reason, we must rethink what it means to "know" God in the first place. In English, the verb *to know* can have multiple meanings, but the two that seem most relevant to our relationship with God is "to hold information in the mind" and "to have encountered." Unfortunately, over the course of Western history, we have tended to claim to know God in the first sense. Religious institutions have maintained their power over us by claiming to have the authority to speak on behalf of God, as though they alone know God's nature and his intentions for us. The Jewish clergy are identified by their teaching role (*rabbi* is usually taken to mean *teacher* in Hebrew), and the primary qualification for leadership in many Islamic sects is scholarly achievement. Even in the Christian tradition, many churches emphasize education as the primary role of the clergy (as a Presbyterian minister, my formal title was Teaching Elder, and I was required to have a master's degree), and the faith is transmitted through instructional tools like the catechism. We equate the teachings of these institutions with religion itself, as though knowledge about God is the same as knowing God.

But if the uncertainty principle shows us that this kind of knowledge is, at best, incomplete and, at worst, misleading, how can we know God in a way that's compatible with that principle? The answer lies in the nature of interpersonal relationships.

I've been married to my wife for over 35 years. I like to think that our relationship is a close one, a relationship in which we've shared with each other as much about ourselves as we dare. I believe I know my wife almost as well as anyone can know someone else. But the nature of that knowledge is surprisingly lacking in factual information. Oh, sure, I know such things as the color of her hair and eyes, the date of her birth, the address of the house she grew up in, and so on. And yet knowing these facts is far from the same as *knowing* my wife. Indeed, someone could learn every*thing* that I know about my wife but still wouldn't know her the way I do. That person wouldn't know what it was like to raise our children together, how sharing even the most routine activities with her is still the highlight of my day, how every dream I have for the future requires her to be there to share it with me.

That's the way we can know God, realizing that our knowledge of God is not based on facts, which are really just illusions anyway, but is based on our relationship with him.

# Finding God in the Probabilistic Universe: Playing the Odds

Newton's discovery of his laws of nature not only changed the way that we view the world, it also changed the way that we view God.

Before Newton, God was thought of as being present and active in the world, in just about everything that happens. Events that people called miracles were amazing because they were rare, not because they had fundamentally different causes than more everyday events.

But the Newtonian view of the universe as a self-sustaining machine turned God into an absentee landlord who made the universe, dropped human beings into it, and then stepped back to allow it to run without further interference. If we accepted miracles at all (and increasingly we didn't), we saw them as rare interventions when God would suspend the physical laws that govern the universe in order to bring about the miraculous event. At its core, though, the world is now viewed as consistently predictable, and that predictability reassures us of the stability of God's providence.

Quantum physics, however, shows us that the world is driven less by unchanging laws and more by the law of averages. What appear to be laws are, in fact, the collected result of a vast number of random events, each of which occurs according to a probability curve (wave function). When these random events combine together, though, they give the appearance of definite laws. The difference is subtle but significant because it provides a bit of wiggle room for God. No longer a matter of laws being suspended, miracles might just be God taking advantage of statistical anomalies that produce a result that would be prevented by absolute laws. Of course, when pushed to its logical conclusion, this would mean that God'isn't really in control of a miracle, just taking credit for some random event, sort of like thinking that you "deserve" to win the lottery. Or maybe there's some middle ground where God takes advantage of the underlying randomness in a way that defies our commonsense understanding of what randomness is.

Quantum physicists insist that subatomic events are truly random, but they also recognize that subatomic events don't become manifest until they are observed, and that the way the event manifests itself depends on the intentions of the observer, as in the double-slit experiment. So maybe God can exploit the intersection of these three phenomena to exert some control over how trillions of subatomic events combine to create a miraculous event. I will admit that most physicists would consider this to be an unacceptable stretch of quantum theory, and yet the new physics itself would have seemed laughably far-fetched to most mainstream physicists only a hundred years ago.

## Finding God in the Empirical Universe: The Fundamental Role of Consciousness

According to the Newtonian worldview, consciousness is merely a byproduct of the activity of neuron cells in the brain. Perhaps as much as anything else, this conclusion from classical physics has weakened religious faith that is inspired by our experience of our own consciousness that we identify with our souls. Our ability to be aware of our surroundings and of our selves (and our awareness of that awareness) leads us to believe that there is something about our existence that mirrors a hidden reality, and that this reality is somehow responsible for the existence of the universe itself. No wonder it disturbs us when science appears to be bent on prying our consciousness away from this hidden reality and even insisting that that it can be explained as the brain just deceiving itself.

But now it appears possible that science and religion might be able to be reconciled after all. This is possible because many quantum physicists recognize that consciousness can no longer be dismissed as just a byproduct of the brain's biochemical activity, but that somehow it has a role that is essential to all reality.

This view comes out of the so-called Copenhagen Interpretation of quantum mechanics. One of the earliest and most influential attempts to understand the weirdness of quantum theory, the Copenhagen Interpretation claims that it is impossible to describe a quantum system apart from the process of measuring its properties. As a result, the role of the observer who performs the measurement is central to how that system becomes "real." This is because that, by choosing what is to be measured, the observer chooses which properties of the system will appear through the process of being measured. More precisely, the range of possibilities that the probability wave represents for a property doesn't collapse to a definite value until the observer takes the measurement.

Maybe this seems to be reading too much into what practically seems to be a self-evident idea. And yet the reading list for this book is filled with the works of respected (that is, not fringe-lunatic) quantum physicists who have been driven to the conclusion that there are "metaphysical" consequences of the discoveries of quantum mechanics. Many mainstream quantum physicists insist that consciousness is an essential ingredient of the processes that produce reality.

Of course, we know that consciousness exists in some form because we happen to possess it, but we also understand that human consciousness is much too puny to be able to play such an ambitious role as being the cause of all quantum events. As a result, there must be a greater consciousness of which ours is perhaps a part or a reflection. In the West, we identify that greater consciousness with God. Whether God is *only* that consciousness or whether this consciousness is merely one dimension of God is open to discussion, of course. But it is clear that the consciousness which is an essential part of the unfolding reality somehow has to do with the God who is the Ground of Being, as Theologian Paul Tillich put it.

Beyond its role in suggesting the possibility of a consciousness that is not just the result of biological processes, quantum mechanics is also being used as the starting point for studies that suggest how the brain can function as a vessel for consciousness. In other words, it appears to provide a scientific basis for theories that support the reality of consciousness. It also suggests how the mechanisms that tie consciousness to the brain provide the means that allow human consciousness to interact with and maybe even flow from the larger consciousness that is the source of our very being.

## Finding God in the Entangled Universe: Rethinking Omnipresence

I suspect that the finding of quantum mechanics that is the most disturbing to those of us who are steeped in the rationalism of the West is the notion of quantum entanglement, the idea that at the quantum level, at least, events are not confined to a specific time and place.

Remember the double-slit experiment? (Of course you do, I keep bringing it up every chance I get.) Particles of light (photons) are fired one at a time at a screen with two slits in it. Even though these particles, being particles, should exist in an incredibly tiny location in space, and even though they exist separated from each other in time, somehow they form an interference pattern behind the screen as though they were waves interfering with each other in the same (much larger) space and at the same time. Quantum theory explains this by saying that a photon (or any other subatomic particle) doesn't really occupy a finite point in space-time until something happens to make it so, such as the attempt to observe the particle. Until then, it exists merely as a range of possibilities called a probability function or a probability wave, because of its wavelike behavior. Until that probability wave collapses to produce a particle with a definite location or momentum (remember the uncertainty principle that says it can't have both!), it's a wave that does not have dimensions, only a range of possibilities of different locations and momenta. Until that probability wave collapses, then, we can only say that a subatomic particle *potentially* occupies time and space. Its existence is not limited by time and space or perhaps even contradicts time and space itself.

As it turns out, the principle of nonlocal quantum entanglement also provides another bridge between science and religion. Traditionally, God has been described as omnipresent, that is, present in every nook and cranny of the universe. Because of the principle of entanglement, this is one of the traditional characteristics of God that is supported by the findings of quantum mechanics. It's much easier to conceive of a God who is able to be present everywhere in a universe where, in a sense, *everything* is omnipresent, or at least potentially present everywhere. The entanglement of the universe provides a context, and maybe even the way, by which God can be thought of as being present everywhere. Taken to its logical conclusion, the principle of nonlocal entanglement suggests that the very notion of space itself is meaningless. To put it another way, the prequantum model of space required God to be "spread out" across the incredible vastness of the universe, a vastness that we are learning is literally beyond comprehension. But quantum theory now shows us that space itself is collapsed so that its extent is no greater than that of a mere photon—or less.

So naturally we have to ask the question of whether God's presence in every part of the universe means that God is identical with the universe: If God is *in* everything, does that mean that mean that God *is* everything? This view of God, which is called pantheism, runs against the Western idea of God's transcendence, the belief that God is separate from his creation even as he fills it. We should be open to reexamining this idea, however, at least so far as the extreme emphasis on how God's separation from the created order doesn't mesh with the quantum picture of the essential unity of everything. Instead of thinking of God as being over against his creation, maybe it would be better to think of God as *containing* the created order, in much the same way that a bottle contains and gives shape to a liquid. This bears further exploration, which we shall do in the next section.

## Finding God in the Holographic Universe: Tying It All Together

I'll bet you won't be surprised to learn that I was a fan of the TV series *Star Trek: the Next Generation.* The starship *Enterprise* of that show seemed to be an idyllic place chock full of technology to meet your every need: a computer that gave you access to all the information and entertainment in the galaxy (the Internet on a much grander scale), food replicators that could create anything you might want to eat or drink, and of course, the amazing holodeck that you could program to recreate just about any environment or storyline you could imagine.

For those of you who might not be familiar with *ST:TNG,* the holodeck was a room where a computer could simulate an entire alternate world populated with landscapes, props, and people, giving the crew member who programmed it a completely immersive experience that seemed every bit as real as, well, the real thing. In one especially compelling episode, Commander Will Riker designs a program that simulates a twentieth-century New Orleans jazz club where he becomes so enchanted by one of the patrons that he almost forgets his duty on the ship beyond the holodeck.

The holodeck has some intriguing similarities to the model of the universe as a hologram that many quantum physicists use to explain quantum principles. What we experience as reality is actually a projection from an underlying, holographic reality. We should be careful not to conclude from this that the hologram is only a simulation, as though the hologram is just a representation of some realer reality. Instead, the hologram that makes up the universe *is* reality, or maybe more exactly, the way that reality *becomes* real. More importantly, unlike the virtual reality created by the computer on the holodeck, the *people* in the hologram are what make the holographic reality truly *real*. In other words, the participation of conscious entities in the hologram is what gives it reality and meaning.

As we try to understand God in this context, we must deal with the question of whether God is the source of the holographic reality (the hologram) or *is* the holographic reality (the projection from the hologram), or something in between. I must admit that I am biased against the idea that we should think of God as the holographic projection rather than the hologram itself or the one who produces it. To view God as the holographic projection reduces him to being the product, rather than the ultimate source, of the holographic projection.

If, on the other hand, God is the hologram, that might provide an explanation of the relationship between the holographic human mind and the mind of God. After all, the Western tradition claims that human beings are filled with the same "stuff" as God. ("God breathed [his spirit] into the human being, and the human being became a living soul," according to Genesis.) It's not so much that we are conscious beings who were created by God at some point in the past. Rather, it is that our consciousness and our being are a projection of the consciousness and being of God, images of God in the same way that a holographic image is a projection of the image stored on the hologram.

I think it's worth noting that if we identify God with the hologram, it's easier to understand the idea of God's transcendence because of the distinction between the hologram and the reality that is projected from the hologram. And so we can come full circle back to the traditional view of God as being the source of the created (projected) order that is not God and yet is the expression of God, a God who extends everywhere (the uniformity of the hologram) and yet is not identical with everything. To my mind, that's a more satisfying view of God and forms a stronger base for a quantum Christian theology.

# PART IV: QUANTUM THEORY AND CHRISTIAN THEOLOGY

.

## The Nature of God

In Part III, we talked about how quantum physics affects our understanding of God in rather general terms, terms that might apply to any monotheistic religious tradition. In Part IV, we will look at the impact that quantum mechanics can have on traditional Christian theology. As we shall see, at times it supports that traditional theology, and at others, it challenges us to revisit that theology. We begin by looking more closely at the Christian notion of God.

There are basically two places to start for a traditional Christian theology: God or self. The second approach is the one that the great seventeenth-century philosopher René Descartes used when he came up with his famous Latin phrase, *cogito ergo sum* ("I think, therefore I am"). He started with the question, What is the one thing that I know for sure? His answer wasn't that God exists, since that could be doubted, but that he (Descartes) exists, and he is sure of that because he is aware of his own thinking. Because I know that I think, Descartes said, I know that I (the one who thinks) must exist. From that point, he followed a chain of reasoning that led him to conclusions about God that just happen to fit with the picture of God endorsed by the Catholic Church of his time. (Surprise!)

Maybe we can admit that the only reasonable way to begin to draw any conclusions about anything (including God) is to begin with the knowledge of our own existence. And yet the problem with this approach is that it ends up defining God in terms that have more to do with

*us* than with God, not the other way around. It turns on
its head the idea that, as Genesis says, "God created [us]
in his own image." Instead, when we start the process
with ourselves, we almost always end up creating God
in *our* image, so to speak.

A theology that draws on insights from quantum
mechanics still can't avoid the need to begin with our
own existence as a starting point, but at least it provides
us with guideposts along the way. These guideposts are
firmly rooted in nature, not just the nature we see
around us (which is easy to romanticize), but nature at
its very foundation, the subatomic level. This is the level
that forms the basis for everything else, the level where
we can assume God is most likely to be found as he
comes into contact with the universe. Quantum physics
helps us understand the basic building blocks which
combine to make up the universe as a whole, the building blocks that God uses to create everything that is. Just
as you can't understand how a clock works unless you
understand how its various parts combine to make the
whole device, you can't understand how the universe
works unless you understand how the little bits, the
particles and fields of quantum mechanics, work together to make up the whole universe. To push the analogy
further (OK, maybe too far), you can understand the
person who designs and builds a clock only if you understand the individual parts of the clock that the person
created to make the clock. (Yep, too far.)

This approach isn't new, of course. Like Descartes, a
lot of theologians have started with nature to get to a
description of the God who—they assume—is responsi-

ble for creating that nature. (Many world religions don't share that assumption, by the way.) The problem with that approach is that they've almost always started at the wrong level, if you will, because they begin with the vastness of the universe and the laws that control how its largest parts behave. They figure that, since galaxies and stars and planets and such stuff all follow laws of motion and gravity that you can describe in rational (mathematical) terms, the God who wrote those laws must be a rational being who put things together in a way that can be understood through logic. A theology that looks at the universe from the *lowest* level, however, discovers a vastly different God, a God who *does* play dice with the universe, despite what Albert Einstein believed.

## Creator/Creation

Besides the philosophical necessity, there's another reason for starting a discussion of God by focusing on his relationship to the universe as its creator. This relationship is also a starting point in the scriptures of the three great monotheistic religions (Judaism, Christianity, and Islam). The book of Genesis, the first book in the Jewish canon, begins with an account of God creating the world, as does the opening verses of one of the Christian gospels (John). The Muslim Koran also alludes to God's role as creator in the second sura (chapter). According to these traditions, because God created the universe, we are to regard him as the Lord of all that is, and that the order which he built into the universe forms the basis of the moral order which should govern our lives as well.

An important aspect of this view of God's creative activity is that we almost always see it as an event that occurred in the distant past, at the very beginning of time. Although the universe is hardly static, we see it as a mostly self-sufficient system that, once it was completed by God, continues to run on its own with little maintenance or interference. Indeed, the relatively few times that we see God injecting himself into the created order we call miracles.

During the last century, a new theological movement has emerged that has a different take on God's role as creator and the nature of creation itself. Grounded in Christianity, process theology holds that rather than being a one-time event that occurred at the dawn of time, creation is instead an ongoing action (process) in which we (all creatures, great and small) participate with God as "co-creators." According to process theology, the universe is not made up of material substances but is instead a sequence of observed events that possess both material and spiritual dimensions. In a sense, then, creation is not an order imposed by God from the outside, but is coaxed into existence through cooperation between God and creation itself.

To a remarkable extent, a theology based on quantum principles closely agrees with the ideas of process theology. Alfred North Whitehead is the philosopher whose writings are the basis of much of process theology. He was a mathematician with a strong interest in physics and may have developed his process philosophy as a reaction to the way Albert Einstein's theories overturned the worldview built on Isaac Newton's law.

While there is little to suggest that Whitehead himself was influenced by quantum mechanics, quantum physicists look to his writings to provide a philosophical framework that helps explain the meaning of much of the "quantum weirdness" that they encounter.

Like process theology, a theology based on quantum principles views the material world, not as a static reality, but as continuously coming into being. Of course, quantum mechanics does speak of a creative event, of sorts, in the Big Bang that started the universe almost 14 billion years ago. Unlike orthodox views of creation, however, this creative event is not a one-time occurrence, but only the first stage in an ongoing process in which every part of the universe is continuously being brought into being through the collapse of the wave functions of elementary particles. As we've seen, one school of thought in quantum mechanics is that a conscious observer plays a crucial role in this collapse, that it doesn't occur until the potential particle is observed (measured). Until that happens, each particle is merely potential, not actualized. Instead of being a collection of particles that were created in the past and have existed since the beginning of time, the material world actually consists of particles that are constantly brought into being through the involvement of a conscious entity. A quantum *theology* identifies this conscious entity with God, the One who constantly calls the world into being.

But wait, you might be saying, all of the experiments that suggest a fundamental role of consciousness involved human observers, not a divine one. True enough, but that's a problem only if, with orthodox Western belief, you insist that God alone can be the creator of the universe. Instead, along with process theology, quantum theology holds that all conscious beings participate in God's creative activity. Later we'll take a closer look at what that means for us.

Before moving on, though, I want to make a point about the essential nature of this created world. We think of this world as being made up of pretty substantial stuff. Imagine holding a rock in your hand. It would seem quite solid to you, dense and hefty. This solidity, however, is misleading. For one thing, as noted in Part II, the atoms that make up the rock are almost completely empty space. If an atom were the size of the earth, for example, the nucleus would be about the size of the Louisiana Superdome. Everything else would be just empty space. Even more oddly, the atoms in the rock don't actually touch the atoms in your hand. The rock doesn't fall through your hand because the atoms in your hand are pressing against the rock's atoms. Instead, the electrical charge of the electrons in the atoms in your hand are repelling the electrons in the atoms in the rock, much like the way two magnets repel each other when you place their negative poles near each other. All of which just points out that there's no meaningful difference between matter and energy. What seems "material" to us is really just condensed energy. (Remember $E=mc^2$?) The world isn't made up of inert stuff; instead, it's vibrating with energy throughout.

## Transcendence/Immanence

The one place where orthodox Christian theology and a quantum theology separate the most is over the idea of God's transcendence, the doctrine that God is separate from and above the universe. According to this teaching, God is so far from and different from the created order that it can't reach him, either to affect him or even know him. This separation is not just a matter of being set apart from the universe in space and time, but also in kind. That is, God's nature is radically different from the nature of the created order. It's beyond a comparison between apples and oranges, it's more on the order of comparing apples and the color orange.

The irony of this doctrine is that it has the effect of limiting God, by placing boundaries that confine God by defining a realm that excludes him. In other words, "in the beginning" God fashioned a province over which he has control, but which he cannot fully enter and be a part of. Whether this was God's choice pretty much doesn't matter; even if it is voluntary, it still imposes limits which defy the idea that God is infinite and omnipresent.

A quantum theology, on the other hand, shares with process theology the idea that creation is an ongoing process where God, in partnership with his creatures, continuously brings the created order into being. God's relationship with his creation has to be understood in terms of this process. While the classical view portrays God has having brought forth the universe and then stepping away from it, as it were, quantum theology portrays God as being intimately present and involved in the very existence of his creation. In the classical view, the created order is, to a very significant degree, self-sufficient. It is possible to conceive of the world as being able to continue on even if God were to withdraw or even "die." From a quantum perspective, on the other hand, the universe depends on the continuous presence and participation of the consciousness that plays an essential role in its ongoing creation.

In a quantum theology, God is separate from the world only to the extent that we can't equate the two, but at the same time, they can't really be considered apart from each other. The relationship of God to the universe is similar to the relationship of the self to the body. Sure, we can imagine ourselves in the abstract as being distinct from our bodies, but it's really hard to hold this image without some sort of compromise, some sort of picture of the self with some kind of body, no matter how insubstantial. Similarly, it is practically meaningless to think of a God who does not express himself through his creation; in a sense, God is as dependent on the universe as the other way around. To put it another way, "God is dead" is impossible so long as the created order exists, and "there is a God" is impossible without the existence of the created order. That means that God is fully immanent in creation, that is, creation is filled with God's presence because creation is the fulfillment of God's existence.

Often the ideas of transcendence and immanence are depicted in opposition to each other, as though one were the negation of the other. That's not necessarily the case, however. It is possible to think of God as being present in, but not of, the universe, pervading it and yet surpassing it. Such a view is consistent with quantum theology, but isn't required by it. What *is* required by quantum theology, however, is that a transcendence that excludes immanence is not possible.

## Trinity

Up to this point, we have been talking about God in terms that would be familiar, if not totally acceptable, to Jews and Muslims, terms that are consistent with the strict, uncompromising monotheism of their traditions. Their faiths insist that God is one and undividable, utterly simple. Orthodox Christianity, however, worships a less simple God, a God who, though one God, exists as three persons, the Father, the Son, and the Holy Spirit.

The doctrine of the Holy Trinity has always been a problem for Christian theology. Like Hollywood wedding vows and the national 55 MPH speed limit of old, it is an idea that has been observed most often in the breach than in the keeping. Some branches of Christianity have chosen to dismiss it altogether—Mormons and Unitarians being perhaps the most obvious—but nearly all others have failed to maintain its spirit by emphasizing one or two of the persons of the Trinity above the others. Most often, the Holy Spirit is the person given the shortest shrift, to the point that the Holy Spirit is almost always referred to in English by an impersonal neuter pronoun (it) rather than by a personal pronoun (he/she).

As an aside, it is important not to fall into the convenient, but wrong, identification of God the Father as being the Creator. Yes, I know that the Apostles' and

Nicene Creeds refer to "God, the Father Almighty, creator of heaven and earth," but classical Trinitarian doctrine identifies creation as being the work of all three
persons of the Trinity. After all, Genesis places the spirit
of God (Hebrew *ruach elohim*) at the scene, hovering over
the face of the waters and playing a decisive role in
giving life to the first human being. Also, the Gospel of
John says that the Son was instrumental in creation:
"Nothing that exists came into being except through
him." It is this very delegation of creation that is most
problematic from the perspective of a quantum theology,
because a quantum theology suggests a God who was
utterly simple before creation. God's "motive" for creation may have been to produce something that God can
relate to; if God is already in relationship through the
interrelationships of the Trinity, there is no apparent
reason for the creation in the first place. We'll talk about
this motive a little later.

At this point, I'm not sure that I can find a way that a
quantum theology can deal with the doctrine of the Holy
Trinity in a way that keeps its historical integrity. Perhaps more capable theologians will be able to do so in
the future. In the meantime, I can at least take comfort in
the fact that even within orthodox circles, the doctrine
has rarely been developed in a way that holds together
logically. Also, I can't resist the temptation to point out
that, much like the ideas of heaven and hell and of the
fall of Satan from heaven, there is really very little biblical warrant for the doctrine. Unlike heaven, hell, and the
fallen angel, though, I won't suggest that the Trinity is
not worthy of belief. I just can't justify it in light of quan-

tum theology, and I wouldn't argue with anyone who still thinks that it's a necessary Christian doctrine. On the other hand, so far as Trinitarian doctrine is an obstacle to dialog with the radical monotheism of Judaism and Islam, I think we should tread very carefully and not insist that it is necessary to the fullness of faith.

Having said all that about the Trinity, however, I think that it's ironic that the Holy Spirit, the most troublesome person of the triune God, is the person of the Trinity who is most easily explained in quantum terms. After all, the Holy Spirit is the mediator, the one who brings God to us and us to God, the one who fills us with God's presence and power and makes us aware of our oneness with God. In many respects, the Holy Spirit is the God of quantum theology, while the other two persons of the Trinity (and the Trinity itself) are but stumbling blocks on our way to reconciling Christian theology with quantum mechanics.

## Human Nature

At first it may seem strange to bring up human nature in a discussion of the nature of God, but it really is necessary. We cannot understand God without reference to his (from our rather narcissistic viewpoint, at least) supreme creation, namely, human beings. The notion that God created us in his image requires us to at least understand who we are so we can view God's image more completely. More to the point, God's significance to us comes in no small part from the fact that God created us for a purpose. To understand God and his purpose, then, we have to know who we are and what *our* purpose for being is.

## Psychology

I have to admit that this is the point where I get the most excited, because it is here that I cease to be a mere accident in the evolution of the vast history of the universe and instead come into my own as a purposeful being.

I use the term "psychology" in the truly classical and philosopical sense, psychology as the study of the human soul (nature), not in the way that the term has been appropriated by science. Psychology is the branch of theology that examines the nature of human beings in relationship to God. In the second creation story of Genesis, God forms the first human being out of lifeless matter but then breathes into him/her, that is infuses him/her with God's spirit, thereby causing the first human being to become a living soul (Hebrew *nephesh*, Greek *psyche*).

The picture of human beings painted by a quantum theology fits remarkably well with the biblical view of human beings. Classical theology holds that human beings are a separate creation from God, that our fundamental nature is of the same order as the material world, separate from God. We are, at most, an image, an imperfect copy of God. A quantum theology and Genesis both hold, however, that we are derived from God, that in essence we are expressions of God within the material world. Our spirit is God's spirit, and apart from that spirit, we have no essential reality.

Quantum theology adds a new twist to this, however, by telling us that we become fulfilled as human beings by being (re)united with God through the work of the God's spirit within us. We are all psychical (that is, animated by the souls given us by God at our creation), but we don't become fulfilled until we find the spirit of God within us.

It is important at this point to make clear that I'm not speaking in allegorical or symbolic terms. When I say that when the spirit of God is present in us, I do not mean that our spirit is *like* God's, or that God's spirit is an adjunct to our essential nature. I believe that a quantum theology (and at its deepest, Christian theology) points us to the reality that we *are* God, that we are the vessels of God's very Godness. Maybe even that for all practical purposes, God is not manifest except in and through us and other conscious beings. This will be made more explicit later when I discuss the notion of Christ's Body, but for now, at least, suffice it to say that there is no clear boundary, no dividing line between us and God. It's not just that God is *in* us, metaphorically speaking, but that God *is* us, and we *are* God.

So then, what exactly are we? If we are one with God, and if God is one, what can account for our experience as distinct, separate selves? Admittedly, this is one area where quantum theory does not speak clearly, so the most I can offer is speculation. Like Descartes, I begin with the fact that I am aware of my own consciousness. From there I infer that because of their resemblance to me, other human beings are also conscious (otherwise, why would I bother writing this book?) and experience themselves as individual selves, just as I do. So the world is filled with conscious human beings. And yet we know that the universe began many billions of years before human beings evolved, and so we must admit that, given the fundamental role of consciousness in bringing the universe into existence, there must be some other form of consciousness besides human consciousness that can account for the existence of the universe around us. The most likely conclusion seems to be that somehow human consciousness emerges from this fundamental consciousness. But how?

At this point I have to use an analogy to illustrate how this might happen. This fundamental consciousness I'm talking about can be compared to water, which pervades the surface and atmosphere of the earth. The vast majority of water exists in huge, undifferentiated pools (lakes and oceans), which can be likened to the fundamental consciousness which forms the basis of universal existence. Sometimes tiny amounts of water separate from these pools through evaporation, form clouds, and then precipitate into droplets of rain or snowflakes. These raindrops or snowflakes keep their separate identity for a while until they fall back to earth and are eventually absorbed into the pools they came from.

If you'll indulge me a bit, I'd like to push the analogy to the point of absurdity, perhaps. As I mentioned, water can be precipitated as snowflakes. One legendary characteristic of snowflakes is that "no two are alike." Our consciousness can be thought of in those terms: each person's consciousness precipitates from the undifferentiated whole and becomes a truly unique, yet fleeting conscious being that eventually returns to the whole (more on this later). We probably could push the analogy yet further by identifying what kinds of conscious beings are more like raindrops, sleet pellets, hailstones, and the like, but that's a path I'd rather not go down at this point. I'll save that for a book that tries to reconcile Christian theology with meteorology.

So what is the reason for this transient isolation into distinct selves? Although quantum physicists have been able to infer the effect of the individual conscious observer on quantum events, they have been unable to account for the existence (much less the nature) of that observer in their models. Again, we have to resort to speculation to account for the presence of conscious individuals. Process theology suggests one possibility, that the "precipitation" of separate conscious entities is a means by which the fundamental consciousness can have experiences that add to its richness and depth. (A beer commercial, of all things, had a great line about The Most Interesting Man in the World: "He lives vicariously, through himself.") When the precipitated consciousness returns to its source, it brings with it the memory of these experiences which then become part of the memories of the whole. This gives a new twist to the Apostle Paul's statement that we are "ambassadors of Christ," doesn't it?

## Sin

No discussion of human nature is complete without looking at the experience of alienation and brokenness that the Bible calls *sin*. At first glance, it might seem that this idea is out of place in the worldview of a quantum theology, but the human condition means that we have to confront sin and understand it in the context of this worldview.

Unfortunately, Christians usually define sin in terms of misdeeds, the breaking of rules that God established to guide our actions. While this has some support in the Bible, it is only a partial view of the larger dynamic of sin as it appears throughout the Bible. The Apostle Paul, in particular, considers sin to be something more basic than just breaking rules. Indeed, he felt free to reject the keeping of the law altogether as the way to be justified before God. For Paul, sin is a state of alienation from God, and the law does little more than highlight and illustrate that alienation. According to Paul, the very fact that we try to reconcile ourselves with God by following the law exposes our estrangement from him. And so God had to take an extraordinary step toward us, becoming incarnate in Jesus and then dying on the cross to show the depth of his love for us and his willingness to accept us as we are.

Sin, therefore, is not an action or even the result of an action, but rather an ongoing condition of being alienated from God. In other words, it's not *what we do*, but *how we are*. In terms of a quantum theology, then, sin is the state of being unaware of our oneness with God and with each other, the haunting illusion that we are isolated, self-sustaining beings on whom no others have a claim. A quantum theology calls us back into relationship with God and with each other, to understand that we are part of a greater whole to which we owe our existence and our faithfulness. The Christian interpretation of quantum theology shows us how the person and work of Jesus Christ can be the way our alienation can be overcome and we can be reconciled to God in Christ.

## Morality and Ethics

If sin isn't the breaking of legalistic rules and God is not a stern judge handing out punishment for breaking those rules, then what is the basis of morality and ethics? If we are the co-creators and, in a sense, centers of our own universe, what obliges us to behave in a way that is not totally self-serving? Well, to be blunt, nothing. But a selfish attitude like this reflects a basic misunderstanding of our nature and our relationship to others: the Golden Rule is not merely a pious injunction, a rule of thumb that provides a practical guide for avoiding conflict. Instead, it is a deep insight into the reality that when we do unto others, we are also doing unto ourselves. It recognizes that all of our actions and attitudes are reflexive, affecting not just others, but ourselves as well. While this is hardly a new way to look at ethical behavior, a quantum theology makes it clearer by showing that our solidarity with each other is not just theoretical or idealistic, but very real. There is no I and thou, only a collective we. True ethical behavior, then, takes into account that neither I nor thou has special claim over the other, but that we must all be given equal consideration in all things.

It is hard for us to live out the Golden Rule in day-to-day life, however, because we feel that we have a greater obligation toward those who are closest to us: our families, our communities, perhaps even our nation. This feeling has a limited validity to the extent that relationships based on cooperation are more effective when they involve those nearest to us. But it is crucial that we recognize that this claim of closeness applies only in matters of sharing and caring. It must never be used as a justification for helping those who are close to us by depriving those who are farther away of the things that they need. We can and must feed our families, of course, but not if it means keeping their bellies full by depriving others of food altogether. Truly ethical behavior means learning to distinguish needs from desires, and it strives to make sure that the needs of all are met before we seek to fulfill our own desires, especially if doing so would keep the needs of others from being met.

## Free will

Mainline science and religion differ sharply on the point of human free will. Most religions insist that we are totally free, in part to justly hold us accountable for our thoughts and actions. In contrast, when it is grounded in the Newtonian worldview, science insists that for every action, there must be a set of prior conditions and events that can account for that action. Free will, therefore, is impossible because it defies the laws of cause and effect upon which science is based, at least at the higher levels where Newtonian laws are in effect.

Quantum mechanics shows that the rules of cause and effect break down at the subatomic level, however. All events are merely the working out of probabilities.

For example, the time it takes a particular atom to decay from one atomic weight to a lesser weight is based on *averages*. While we can say with a fair degree of certainty that a given percentage of an isotope will decay to a lighter form in $x$ days, we cannot make the same prediction for a single atom. It could take $2x$ days, or it could take $x/2$ days. Of course, the greater the separation in time before or after the average, the lower the probability, so it tends to work out that it is most likely that the atom will shed its neutron around the time that is predicted by the average.

What science hasn't satisfactorily explained, however, is what prompts a particular atom to shed its neutron when it does. It is almost as though the atom chooses to drop its neutron early or to hang on to it beyond the average decay time. Of course, it's hard to imagine an atom as having the sophistication to exercise a real choice, but the point of this is to show that there is room, perhaps even a requirement, for free will in the underlying functioning of the universe. Perhaps the atom itself isn't choosing when to decay, but perhaps that choice is being made for it by some higher consciousness.

Assuming that this higher consciousness is God, then, we can see that if God has free will, then we must as well, since we are individual expressions of God in the material world. Granted that it's a free will derived from God, but it is very real and, in its own way, quite independent. Our freedom is a reflection, a manifestation of God's will within the realm over which we ourselves hold sway. Rather than seeking to submit our will to God's will, therefore, our responsibility is to choose on behalf of God. That means that we are utterly, awesomely accountable for our actions because we cannot fall back on the excuse that we were only following orders or worse yet, a program.

## Afterlife

There are some who say that the whole purpose of our lives is to determine whether we will spend the rest of eternity in heaven or in hell, as though all of life is but a one-question, pass/fail test. There are several problems with this idea, however. The first is that such an idea is not very biblical. Heaven and hell as destinations for human souls is nowhere to be found in the Bible. The Jewish Scriptures (the Old Testament of the Christian Bible) have only a few traces of belief in an afterlife, and that afterlife (a shadowy semi-existence in the underworld) is not something to seek after. This is shown clearly by the fact that, as late as Jesus' day, the most conservative Jews, the Sadducees, rejected belief in resurrection from the dead as unbiblical. On the other hand, the New Testament sides with the Pharisees, the more progressive(!) Jews of Jesus' day. It does so by promising that the righteous will, at the end of time, be raised to a glorious and eternal life, while sinners will be left to lie a-mouldering in their graves. In the New Testament, as in the Old, heaven is the place where God dwells, and the presence of human souls there is an extraordinary (and symbolic) exception in the book of Revelation. But overall, the New Testament talks about resurrection as being the reward for a faithful life.

From the perspective of a quantum theology, however, the very idea of "life after death" is mistaken, for it assumes that life is the primary, the true existence and what comes after life is secondary and even uncertain. For a quantum theology, the manifest, material world is just a reflection of an underlying, eternal reality. The question is not whether there is life after death, but rather what our existence is like before and after our sojourn in the manifest world. That is a question that cannot be answered with certainty by a quantum theology, but as we suggested earlier, it seems likely that we as individuals will cease to be individuals. Instead, we will be reunited with God and returned to the state of oneness from which we temporarily emerged to partake of this life. Buddhism calls this state *nirvana*.

The problem for those of us who want to understand quantum theology in terms of Christian theology, however, is that this state is the exact opposite of what the Bible portrays. Traditional Christianity promises (or threatens!) an eternal existence of the individual. Christian doctrine tells us that after death, God judges each of us and rewards the righteous and punishes the unrighteous accordingly. Because a quantum theology suggests that we don't persist as individuals for eternity, this presents a problem: What's the point of judging us when our ultimate fate doesn't depend on the outcome of that judgment? As suggested earlier, perhaps the imagery of a trial is misplaced, and a better way of viewing what happens after death is more like an employee performance review. (OK, maybe that's not much of an improvement.) Instead of being judged by a disapproving or even wrathful God, I prefer to believe that when we return to the fundamental consciousness, we will be given the opportunity to replay our life experiences and the choices we made along the way, all to contribute to the depth of understanding of those experiences as they are added to the collective memory. The stakes of that process are certainly less far-reaching than that of the traditional judgment, and yet somehow it seems more worthwhile (not to mention more just) than determining my eternal fate based on my behavior during what amounts to an infinitesimally tiny span of time.

When I think of the fairness of this "system" of judgment and reward/punishment, I'm drawn to thinking about recent trends in the American justice system. Increasingly, children who commit serious crimes are being tried as adults, sometimes children as young as 12 years of age or less. This despite the fact that the vast majority of child psychologists know that children that age haven't reached a stage of development where they can understand the moral dimensions of what they've done. Ironically, it seems that this is most likely to happen when the crime is particularly heinous, even though children are actually less likely to understand the severity of such crimes because they are outside of their normal frame of reference. In other words, a child is more likely to be able to understand that stealing a candy bar is wrong, because they know what it's like to be stolen from, than how killing someone is wrong. It just seems manifestly unfair to hold children accountable for the rest of their lives for a decision that they can barely understand. For me, the same thing applies to the idea of us being judged for eternity for actions that we take while we are "growing up" in this life. Few of us have reached a level of ethical maturity to fully understand the implications of what we think and do, and so it would seem unfair (and quite pointless) to send us to heaven or hell for eternity because of those choices.

## Our Relationship with God

An important feature of Western religions is their emphasis on God as a personal God. That not only means that God is a person, but also that each of us has a unique, personal relationship with God. In the Western tradition, then, God can't be fully understood apart from this personal relationship.

### Worship

While at first it might seem strange to talk about worshipping a God who is in each of us, it's strange only if you believe that God somehow needs our praise to make him feel better about himself. In fact, any highly developed religious belief holds that worship is less about making God feel appreciated and more about making us aware of our dependence on and love for the one who creates, sustains, and saves us, and then expressing that awareness through ritual. Worship serves the same purpose for Christians whose beliefs are shaped by a quantum theology: through the rituals of worship, we allow ourselves to be drawn closer to God, that is, to realize our unity with him. If we were free from sin, free from the illusion of being separate from

God, we would have no need of worship. But since we are only vaguely aware of our true nature, it is necessary for us to at least begin our devotions by addressing God as "thou," until we can break through the barriers that separate us. As the Apostle Paul wrote, "For now we see as through a glass, darkly, but then we shall see face to face."

Christian worship takes an astonishingly wide range of forms, including the simple, musically oriented "praise" services of Protestant evangelicalism, the fervent enthusiasm of Pentecostalism, and the highly structured liturgies of traditional churches. None of them, of course, reflect a viewpoint based on quantum theology, but I don't think it's necessary to revise them to do so. Instead, I think it would be better to allow them to stand as a lens through which we can view quantum theology, to add emotional and spiritual depth to what might otherwise be a rather dry, abstract perspective on Christian faith. Quantum theology needs worship to give those who follow it a way to experience God's presence and love, not just think about it in theoretical terms.

There is one aspect of worship that is particularly useful to us in this regard: It is a group experience, as opposed to the private devotions of a solitary believer. It's this communal experience that reminds us that our relationship with God isn't just a personal, I-Thou encounter, but is an experience that can best be shared with and through others. Group worship reminds us that we share our relationship to God with others, none of whom has a greater or lesser claim to God's attention than any other.

## Lordship

If I am God (or at least a bit of him), then why should I regard God as Lord? In a way, citizenship in a democracy presents the same sort of incongruity: The people separately and together are sovereign, so why can't I exercise my sovereignty by refusing to obey laws with which I disagree? (That's the root of civil disobedience, after all.) But the key is the idea that people are sovereign separately *and* together. That is, to make democracy work we must submit our sovereignty as individuals to the sovereignty of the majority; otherwise, democracy dissolves into anarchy. God's Lordship is of a like nature: although I am radically free as an individual manifestation of God, I must also recognize the importance of aligning myself, harmonizing my will to God. God's Lordship is not coercive, but persuasive, and based on love, not threat of punishment.

Of course, God's Lordship has much more to it than his authority over us as individuals; it also has to do with God's relationship to all of creation. As its source, God has a special role (responsibility, even) for sustaining that creation. That means that, as members of the collective whole that is God, we share with him that responsibility for the world that he and we have created. And so we find ourselves back in the Garden of Eden, where God gave the first human being the job of tending it. God's delegated Lordship over his creation means that we are called to protect it from our own exploitation and neglect.

## Discipleship

Being a disciple means to be a student, a learner. Jesus' disciples were those who recognized him as rabbi, a teacher, and submitted themselves to learning from him. Discipleship involves submission, allowing ourselves to listen to a teacher and then to incorporate the teacher's insights into our own beliefs and actions. It requires recognition of our individual limitations and that others might not be bound by those same limitations. It doesn't mean that we must uncritically accept the teacher's authority. Instead we must learn how to integrate the teacher's insights into our lives while maintaining our personal responsibility for our own ideas and beliefs.

Discipleship for quantum Christians is not especially different. We acknowledge that, in our present state, our knowledge and our love are imperfect, and our purpose for existing in the world is to move ourselves toward perfection. To that extent, then, discipleship is our true reason for being, to gain a greater experience of what it means to love fully and unconditionally, and to share that experience with others, in this life and when we return to the our place of origin.

Christians, of course, are called to be disciples of Jesus Christ. Such discipleship means, above all, looking to how Jesus speaks to us through the Bible and through the community of Christian believers, seeking his counsel as all Christians do, but looking at that counsel with eyes tuned by the insights of a quantum theology. That means paying special attention when we hear Jesus calling us to love and forgive each other, to share what we've received from each other with each other, and to treat each other as we would be treated ourselves.

## Law

Given that a quantum theology leads us toward a view of God as loving and persuasive rather than judgmental and punitive, it is hard to understand what role divine law might have in such a view. And yet, as Christians, we stand in a tradition that continues to recognize the fundamental validity of that law.

The term *law* has multiple meanings, of course. One sense is that of a *physical law,* that is, a description of how physical things always behave. I believe that it is significant that quantum mechanics has demonstrated that these laws do not actually apply at all levels, that at the quantum level not only are these laws not "enforced," they are consistently broken. This should serve to remind us that no law is absolute and can at most be viewed as a way of thinking about the way that the world behaves.

The more relevant meaning of *law,* however, is as a rule to guide human behavior that is imposed and enforced by an external authority, such as God. Unlike physical laws, these laws are binding on us only to the extent that when we break them, we are subject to punishment after the fact, usually after a judgment has been reached that we broke the law in a way that deserves conviction and punishment.

Because Christians who follow a quantum theology believe that God is within us and is not a detached authority, we might be tempted, like the Galatians that the Apostle Paul wrote to, to reject any and all obligation to obey God's laws. We recognize that we are not bound by arbitrary ,laws that would tell us what we are not to eat or wear, and certainly some laws (such as those that sanction slavery or prescribe death for a woman who is raped but does not cry out) are even abhorrent to us in the modern world. Yet we must also recognize that, as culture-bound as such laws are, they reflect principles that must be discerned and at least considered as a template for our actions. The law, then, provides a guide (in Paul's words, a pedagogue) for how we relate to God, our neighbor, and ourselves. It expresses our highest ideals and applies those ideals to specific situations and actions. It is up to us to choose how to act in response to the law, recognizing that we are the ones responsible for its interpretation and, in a sense, its enforcement.

## Prayer

Like much of our religious lives, prayer has often been a stumbling block for the spiritually immature. For some of us, it's a tacit admission that we don't really believe in a God who knows all, a God who needs us to tell him what's really happening and to suggest how he should respond. For others, it seems pointless since God does know everything and hardly needs us to draw his attention to it.

The usual escape from these traps has been to view prayer as a means of self-development and for drawing closer to God by intentionally engaging him in dialog. For a quantum Christian, this is a good start toward a fuller understanding of prayer, but it doesn't take into consideration the reality that we are not truly separate from God, that our selves and our consciousness are already one with God. As we've always suspected (feared?), prayer is just us talking to ourselves—not in the sense that we are not communicating with an other, but in the sense that through prayer we seek to get beyond the illusion of separation and re-establish our communion with our true self, with God. Prayer is the attempt of the individual soul to take up the dialog which was the motive for creation in the first place and in that way to harmonize our individual existence with the eternal whole of which we are a part.

## Reason

Quantum theology proposes that God is discovered through rational processes, radically so, in fact, because the equations of quantum physics draw us to the conclusion that a higher consciousness of some sort exists. It would seem as though we do not need more than reason to recognize God and his role in the coming into being of the material world.

In a sense, this is true. But it must also be admitted that throughout history people who have been convinced of God's existence and believed that they have knowledge and even a relationship with him reached that conclusion by means other than the rigors of mathematical analysis. If physicists, mystics, and prophets have all managed to reach the same conclusion, then there must be some validity to the methods used by all three. That is, God must have chosen to reveal himself, however imperfectly, through means other than through the laws of the natural world. Revelation and reason must both be accepted as valid, yet incomplete, ways to discover God.

Up to this point, we have relied on the rational to provide the path to this discovery. We should at least pause, however, to recognize and appreciate the role that other time-honored methods of God's self-disclosure must play in helping us develop a fuller understanding of who he is.

## Revelation

Throughout history, God has been portrayed as being hidden, and we have been allowed to glimpse him only through exceptional revelation. In some cases, that revelation has been handed down by specially designated prophets and seers, while in others such revelation has been viewed as available to all people, if only they would look hard enough or apply the correct method or attitude. Even among those who seek God using rational methods, natural and mathematical laws have been regarded as a way God discloses himself. Inevitably, of course, this revelation has been filtered through the cultural and psychological context of the people who have given that revelation. As a result, that revelation has been so shaped by this context that it is difficult to find the revelation of God in the midst of the psychological and cultural dross which inundates it. To a certain extent, a quantum theology can act as a tool to help us drill through the cultural layers to get to the core truths. But rational theology must also be careful not to be too quick to discard anything that cannot be demonstrated by scientific means, repeating the mistakes of the reductionists. Instead, a quantum theology must learn to appreciate the role that God's more active self-revelation can play in helping us "flesh out" his character.

## Scriptures

Especially in the Judeo-Christian-Muslim traditions, God is understood to have chosen to reveal himself most authoritatively and reliably through the writings of specific prophets and sages, to the point that God is considered to be the author of those books, at least to a certain degree. Thus scriptures play a crucial role in these traditions as they seek to know God and to understand our obligations toward him.

Quantum theology must be careful not to underestimate the role that such scriptures play in bringing us to a fuller understanding of God. Indeed, where quantum theology and the Bible are at odds, the quantum Christian must approach such differences with caution, realizing that there might be an underlying harmony that is not readily discernible. Even when such a harmony cannot be found, the quantum Christian must not cavalierly dismiss the authority of the writings that seem to contradict the quantum view of God and humanity. After all, if a photon can be both a quantum (particle) and a wave, then contradictory portrayals of God might be equally useful in understanding God.

Perhaps more to the point, the scriptural revelation of God can give us clues about how to respond to God in ways that the relative aridness of quantum theology cannot. By placing God at the center of an epic story, God is given a role in human history that would be difficult if not impossible to divine (sorry) from quantum equations and theories. Such is the power of myth, a power that cannot be ignored as long as we inhabit this mortal state.

If we don't discard or neglect scriptures as a way of understanding God and ourselves, then a quantum theology can prove valuable as a guide to understanding those scriptures. Imagine what a quantum interpretation might be of God's words in Genesis, "Let *us* create...." How might a quantum Christian understand Jesus' statement that he "did not come into this world to condemn it, but to save it" or that the Kingdom of God is within you (or in your midst). How are we to understand the Apostle Paul's rejection of those "who turn the truth of God into lies and who worship and serve the creation instead of the creator"? As quantum Christians, we must not turn away from scripture simply because we assume that it no longer speaks to us; instead, we should embrace it and strive to find its deeper meaning that can be brought out by the insights of a quantum theology.

## Myth

As we draw upon scriptures to help us draw a clearer picture of God and our relationship to him, it is vital that we do not fall into the trap of allegorizing them, of trying to reduce them to a collection of symbols that stand in for the "facts" of a quantum theology. The power of the creation stories in Genesis do not lie in the fact that God's initial creation of light "represents" the elemental nature of energy in creation, for example. Instead, the stories must be taken as a whole and, in a sense, at face value. The power and meaning of the stories of scripture do not lie in their details, but in our response to them. In that way, they work much like Jesus' parables. When Jesus told the story of the prodigal son, for example, he wasn't using the sons to represent any "real" persons or groups. Instead, he was seeking to stir up a response in his hearers, who were most likely scandalized by the father's willingness to overlook the immoral actions of his rebellious son and by his apparently heartless indifference to the faithful, but jealous, brother. The purpose was to get the hearers to react and then look inward at that reaction to gain a clearer insight into their ability to place love ahead of conventional notions of right and wrong.

As we use scripture, then, we must be careful to respect its mythic character and allow ourselves to be moved by the power of the narrative, rather than giving in to the temptation to subject them to an analysis that produces little more than meaningless parts. Again, as quantum Christians, we must not allow the rational basis of our worldview to cause us to overlook the power of revelation that is found in story and poetry.

## Faith

A common fallacy held by both believers and scientific seekers of truth is that faith and reason are somehow at odds with each other, at such opposite poles that we cannot approach one without moving away from the other. Because of this fallacy, many people who promote a scientific approach to the discovery of God insist that the scientific method has to exclude any role for faith in the process of discovery.

Excluding faith in this way would be naïve, however, because doing so fails to appreciate the role that faith plays in all human endeavor. Indeed, the reliance on the scientific method itself is based on faith, a belief that this particular method is a more reliable way to find the truth than any other method. Certainly, the effectiveness of that method has been consistently supported by its results over the past several centuries, but the expectation that this method will continue to be equally reliable in the future is a matter of faith. Indeed, it is a matter of faith to suppose that the subject of the scientific method is reality when it could just be an incredibly coherent illusion instead.

Faith is fundamental to all human activity. Sometimes scientific rationalism can support the soundness of faith, and sometimes it can point out where that faith is misdirected. But it cannot substitute for faith, much less eliminate it altogether. A quantum theology, therefore, must use the scientific method as a technique for refining faith, not to surmount it. On the other hand, those whose understanding of God is based solely on faith must also accept how fragile their position is, and they must accept that faith and science can and should work together to create a fuller picture of God than either approach can by itself.

## Truth

Perhaps one of the most disconcerting conclusions of the new physics is that truth is not unitary, in other words, there is no such thing as a single truth, even at the most basic level. Light is both wave and particle, and an event doesn't become real until it is "forced" into being by observation. When a traveler moves extremely fast, time slows down compared to the passage of time experienced by a stationary observer. Objects in our everyday experience obey very different laws than those that apply to objects at the subatomic level or to objects that travel at great speeds.

For those of us who were raised to believe in absolutes, such "truthiness" is hard to accept. If there can be more than one truth in a matter, then how can we know what is real? How can we avoid sliding down the dangerous slope of intellectual and moral relativism in which the truth ends up being only what is the most convenient for us?

Well, we can't. Instead, we must make our own choices and live with the consequences, rather than ceding our freedom to an external and perhaps even arbitrary authority. More importantly, we are no longer justified in imposing our choices on others in the name of a truth that just happens to coincide with our interests.

As a logical category, truth has been dethroned. While it might prove useful on occasion to describe the relative usefulness of a particular bit of data, it can no longer be relied upon as the final arbiter of reality. We are ultimately responsible for creating our own truth, which may or may not coincide with others' truths. Fundamentally, reality is at most a consensus. Of course that's frightening, but it should feel eerily familiar to anyone who has sat in a college dorm in a cloud of smoke and grappled with the challenge, "Oh, yeah? Prove to me that you exist."

## Miracles

One of the most intriguing implications of quantum theology is that not only are miracles possible within a scientific framework, they are practically inevitable. Under the dominance of Newton's laws of nature, miracles have been thought of as impossible suspensions of those laws. Quantum mechanics, however, has replaced the certainties of physical laws with the fuzziness of chance. Rather than knowing for certain that a particular particle will be in a particular location at a certain time, as Newton and Einstein would expect, quantum theory asserts that the most we can know is that there's a certain probability that the particle will be in a particular place at a particular time, but there's also a possibility that the particle could appear literally anywhere else. It may be much less likely that the particle would appear, say, one inch away from where it is most likely to appear, but that cannot be ruled out with certainty.

What we have traditionally regarded as immutable laws, therefore, are actually the result of a great accumulation of probable events. More skeptical quantum physicists would assert that the probability of even a few atoms, for example, appearing somewhere other than predicted is so infinitesimally small as to be meaningless. But they cannot say that it is flatly impossible.

So even they would have to admit that there's a very tiny amount of wiggle room for the possibility of a miracle, that is, an event that is highly improbable. What intrigues me, then, is the possibility that the fundamental consciousness (God) has the ability to load the dice, as it were. After all, if it is God who establishes the probability of each event occurring, is it truly inconceivable that God can take advantage of that mechanism to bring about unexpected results?

The picture of the universe painted by quantum physics is already so strange as to defy rational acceptance. It really is not much of a stretch, at least for an open mind, to accept the possibility that it might be even a little bit stranger than we thought.

## The Quantum Christ

The idea behind this book is that a theology based on the insights of quantum mechanics can revitalize and renovate Christian theology for the twenty-first century. Of course, that means that it must be able to explain the life, death, and resurrection of Jesus and make them meaningful. Jesus, of course, is crucial to Christian theology, and a Christian quantum theology must be able to account for his central position for the faith.

### Incarnation

Perhaps *the* most fundamental belief of orthodox Christianity is the doctrine of the incarnation, that Jesus was the unique Son of God, God made flesh to live among us and to die for us. It is also at this point where a quantum theology most clearly challenges orthodox Christianity, because a quantum theology suggests that we all are manifestations of God and that since we occupy material bodies, we are all incarnations of God. In order to have a truly Christian quantum theology, we must be willing to confront this tension and somehow find a way to understand the uniqueness of Christ's incarnation even as we acknowledge our own nature as material manifestations of God.

Maybe one way to resolve this tension is by recognizing that God's appearing in Christ was uniquely powerful and complete, that the early church saw in Christ the presence of God in a way that is not evident in the lives of others. In other words, Christ's reflection of God was clearer, more enlightening than the dim lights that struggle to shine through the rest of us. So it is less that Christ alone was an embodiment of God than that his being provided a more complete revelation of the nature of God.

Another approach might be to regard Christ's incarnation as being archetypal. In other words, while the incarnation of the Christ might not have differed in nature from our own incarnation, as it were, it was the first hint of what human nature truly is and is to become. Just as we see Jesus' death and resurrection as the precursor of the resurrection of the faithful, so might we see his incarnation as a sign to us of our present nature.

Once we deal with the issue of the uniqueness of Christ's incarnation, however, we can see that a quantum theology helps clarify how that incarnation can be explained in a way that Christian doctrine has been unable to accomplish before. By dissolving the artificial distinction between God and the material world, a quantum theology shows how God can fully inhabit the manifest order in a way that was impossible because of the now-obsolete narrow view of God's transcendence. Christ's incarnation now is not only possible, it is an essential aspect of the divine and the physical realms.

## The Jesus of history

A common tendency in Christianity is to lose sight of the fact that Jesus of Nazareth was a very human being who walked the dusty roads of Palestine, who grew weary and hungry, and who could even lose his temper on occasion. In that way, he was very much like us, even though he carried a kernel of divinity (just as we do). As suggested earlier, Jesus was not different from you and me in kind, but only in degree: Within the limitations imposed by his historical, cultural, and religious context, he was more aware of and more able to act upon his connection to God than we can. Contemporary Christian scholars have not been able to clearly establish how self-aware Jesus was of his Sonship, and so we should not be surprised that it's not really clear how much he understood about the relationship between his existence in the physical world and his connection to God. But I find it easy to believe that, even if he was not fully enlightened on this point, he had a much stronger intuition of the matter than just about anyone else, at least among those within the Jewish strand of religions. (Considering how much overlap there is between the worldview of Hinduism/Buddhism and of a quantum theology, though, I suspect that Gautama Buddha had a pretty good idea as well.)

Talking about the historical Jesus is not just to recognize that Jesus existed within human history (in a way that is different from the way that Buddha or Moses can be considered historical persons), but also that *his* history was tied up with the larger human history in a unique way. In other words, the drama of his life, in particular his crucifixion, resurrection, and ongoing presence in and through the church, have had an impact on human history unparalleled by any other religious figure.

## Crucifixion

The cross is literally crucial to Christianity, and yet it is one of the hardest aspects of Jesus' life to understand. Jesus' death on the cross proved to be "folly to the Gentiles and a stumbling block to the Jews," as the Apostle Paul put it. Many theories have been offered to make sense of the event, ranging from the claim that Jesus was the perfect sacrifice to appease an angry God, to the more abstract idea that Jesus' giving himself up for execution showed his radical obedience to God, Jesus sort of carrying through Isaac's willingness to offer his life to God at the hands of his father Abraham.

Given the central role that love played in Jesus' ministry, however, the crucifixion must be understood as an expression of that love. Jesus loved us so much that he was willing to lay down his life in such a dramatic and public manner to prove that death is not final, ultimately not real, and the magnitude of his love can be measured by the humiliation and suffering he was willing to endure to show the depths of that love.

From a quantum theological perspective, the crucifixion cannot stand alone, however. Unlike such doctrines as substitutionary atonement, a quantum theology insists that the crucifixion itself is meaningless except as the prerequisite for the resurrection.

## Resurrection

Interestingly, while the church throughout the centuries has struggled to understand the crucifixion, it has had no such difficulty with Christ's resurrection, being content to accept it on face value as a happy fact. A quantum theology, of course, cannot be quite so blithe, considering that the historical understanding of the resurrection is as a literally physical event. Jesus' physical body was laid in the tomb, and it was that physical body that was restored to life on the third day. Given quantum theology's insistence on the secondary nature of physical reality, it is difficult to give the physical resurrection of Jesus the leading place that it has in orthodox Christianity.

On second thought, though, it is hard to imagine a clearer picture of the radical freedom of someone who has discovered that death is an illusion than how the Bible describes the risen Christ. Having made the round trip from the manifest physical realm to the unmanifest, and then back to the physical world, Christ finds himself freed of the constraints which bind the rest of us who continue to be confined here. He is able to pass through locked doors, conceal his identity at will, and even (if you will pardon such a prosaic interpretation of the ascension) to fly. In his death and resurrection, Jesus has managed to travel to and return from that "undiscovered country" which is the reality that underlies the illusory physical world, and he has come back to give us a hint, a sample of what that reality is. If you ignore the quantum-inspired vocabulary, I think you must agree that even orthodox Christianity could not argue with that interpretation.

## The Body of Christ

While it is indisputable that Jesus is the central subject of the Christian scriptures, it is also noteworthy that fully half of the New Testament is devoted to recounting the stories about and providing direction to the early church after his death and resurrection. All the gospels agree that Jesus intended his ministry to continue beyond his earthly life, and so in varying ways commissioned and empowered his followers to carry on his ministry.

In the New Testament, a recurring metaphor for the church is that it is the body of Christ. From a quantum perspective, however, this is more than a metaphor, but rather a very powerful reality. As manifestations of the same God of whom Christ was the special incarnation, we are uniquely aware of our oneness with that God and with each other. This oneness is reinforced by our partaking in the sacraments through which we participate in Christ's death and resurrection, making them real in our own lives. Thus, being members of Christ's body is not a means to an end (salvation), but is salvation itself, the acceptance and fulfillment of our true nature as individual manifestations of the universal consciousness we call God.

# A Concluding Unscientific Postscript[*]

Well, there you have it, the first attempt (that I know of) to rethink Christianity in light of quantum physics, a Quantum Christianity, if you will. For some of you, I suspect that I've stripped away so much of Christian orthodoxy that it barely resembles the "faith of our fathers" that you grew up with or around. For others, I'm sure that I've been willing to hang on to too many traditional beliefs to really bring Christianity into the twenty-first century. Oh, well. At least I tried.

But what, exactly, is it that I tried to do? One thing I *didn't* try to do was to convert you to my way of thinking. While I've found the ideas about Christianity and science that I've presented in this book both exciting and intriguing, I must admit that they are just barely formed. Far from a complete and coherent picture of what a Quantum Christianity could be, this book is at best a sketch of the promise of such a vision. It would be rash of me to expect you to adopt a belief system that I myself have just begun to incorporate into my own worldview.

So please understand that if this book has upset you (and if that's the case, you probably wouldn't have gotten this far anyhow), I don't want you to think that I

---

[*] My apologies to Danish Philosopher Søren Kierkegaard for (mis)appropriating this title. And my apologies to you for breaking my promise not to use footnotes.

have sought to undermine what you believe, much less to replace it. I just wanted to give you another way to look at what you believe, perhaps to give you an opportunity to deepen your faith, even if that happens because you've found new reasons to believe as you do despite yet another assault by science.

On the other hand, I also hope that you don't reject the ideas in this book out of hand just because they don't line up with current orthodoxy. One of the most stinging (and true!) criticisms directed against people of faith is that we tend to cling to irrational beliefs in the face of compelling evidence to the contrary. This book has tried to show that the apparent clash between faith-based and fact-based worldviews is false, that there might be a scientific basis for faith, and even a spiritual substance to science. If your biases prevent you from considering that possibility, then I guess I've failed.

But if your mind is open enough to at least entertain this possibility, I invite you to join the conversation at http://quantumxpianity.blogspot.com. Come to add your insights, whether they support my thesis or poke holes in it. All I really want is for folks to begin talking about the ideas and fallacies I've presented in this book. If that happens, then I've succeeded, regardless of where the conversation ultimately leads.

# READING LIST

This isn't a comprehensive biography by any means. And I don't even necessarily claim that I relied on all of these books to help me develop the ideas in this book. I did read them, however, and found enough in them that I thought you might find them useful for learning more about quantum physics and Christian theology.

*The Dancing Wu Li Masters: An Overview of the New Physics,* by Gary Zukav. Published by Perennial, an imprint of HarperCollins Publishers, New York. This book is a classic introduction to the new physics that features a unique blending of profundity and levity. *Wu li* is the Chinese name for physics, but it has a number of other meanings that Zukav uses to illuminate the deeper implications of the new physics.

*The Fabric of the Cosmos: Space, Time, and the Texture of Reality,* by Brian Greene. Published by Vintage Books, New York. Brian Greene, the author of *The Elegant Universe,* is one of the best explainers of physical science for a popular audience, and this book lives up to his reputation. If you want to learn just about everything you can about the new physics, including the controversial quantum string theory that I was too squeamish to touch upon, this is the book for you.

*How We Believe: Science, Skepticism, and the Search for God,* by Michael Shermer. Published by Henry Holt and Company, New York. I include this book mainly as

one of the better examples of how those who adhere
to the classic scientific worldview deal with religious
experience by reducing it to a mere neurological
process. Shermer is the founding publisher of *Skeptic*
magazine.

*The Mind of God: The Scientific Basis for a Rational World,*
by Paul Davies. Published by Simon & Schuster,
New York. This book looks for meaning in the way
that the laws that govern the universe reveal a deeper meaning to the very existence of that universe
and how that meaning is based on the fact that
through the evolution of consciousness, the universe
has made itself self-aware.

*Omnipotence and Other Theological Mistakes,* by Charles
Hartshorne. Published by the State University of
New York Press, Albany. Hartshorne examines the
deficiencies of traditional views of God and presents
interesting alternatives to such classical divine at-
tributes as omnipotence, omniscience, and infallibil-
ity. Not a book for those who prefer to stick to past
certainties, but liberating to those who seek a broad-
er (and perhaps more believable) understanding of
God.

*The Physics of Consciousness*, by Evan Harris Walker.
Published by Perseus Publishing, Cambridge. This
is the book that started it all for me. It weaves a de-
tailed analysis of the role that quantum mechanics
plays in the neural mechanisms of the brain that un-
derlie consciousness, along with reminiscences of

the dying of a childhood friend/girlfriend and insights derived from Zen Buddhism.

*The Process Perspective: Frequently Asked Questions about Process Theology,* by John B. Cobb, Jr. Published by Chalice Press, St. Louis. Though it developed independently, process theology (a branch of process philosophy) shares much with the worldview that emerges from quantum philosophy. This is an excellent introduction to process theology that might help you ground the ideas in my book in a more systematic theology.

*Quantum Theology: Spiritual Implications of the New Physics,* by Diarmuid O'Murchu. Published by The Crossroad Publishing Company, New York. O'Murchu is a priest and social psychologist who has written a number of books on spirituality. The first part of this book provides a very good introduction to the tension between the scientific and religious worldviews. The rest of the book focuses on the spiritual implications of this tension but only touches on classical Christian beliefs in passing. Still, it's a very good book if you want to dig into the impact of quantum theory on spiritual formation.

*Science and Theology: An Introduction,* by John Polkinghorne. Published by Fortress Press, Minneapolis. Written by a physicist who also happens to be an ordained priest of the Church of England, this book provides an excellent, if rather dense, survey of the subject of science and religion.

*The Self-Aware Universe: How Consciousness Creates the Material World,* by Amit Goswami, with Richard E. Reed and Maggie Goswami. The Goswamis and Reed have produced a very approachable survey of quantum physics and its implications for our understanding of the universe and ourselves. This is one of the first books you should read if you're looking for a clearer understanding of the relationship between quantum theory and the role of consciousness in the emergence of the universe.

*Taking the Quantum Leap: The New Physics for Non-Scientists, by Fred Alan Wolf.* Published by Harper and Row, New York. This is an excellent and entertaining review of the history and theories of the new physics, and how those theories affect how we see our world and ourselves. Reading this book is a great way to get deeper into quantum mechanics.

*The Tao of Physics: An Exploration of the Parallels between Modern Physics and Eastern Mysticism,* by Fritjof Capra. Published by Shambhala Publications, Boston. Capra does a great job of laying out the essentials of the new physics and relating them in detail to the teachings of Taoism, one of the ancient religions of China. It's almost scary how Taoism anticipated much of how the new physics would come to view the universe, and Capra's book helps us understand how Eastern traditions are much better prepared to cope with the implications of science than is the case with the great monotheistic religions.

*The Universe in a Single Atom: The Convergence of Science and Spirituality,* by the Dalai Lama. Published by Broadway Books, New York. Orthodoxy is an idea almost peculiar to Western religions, and the Dalai Lama shows why Eastern religious traditions are able to adjust more readily to worldviews derived from the new physics. For the Dalai Lama's Buddhism, the challenge presented by science is not how to defend Buddhism against science's onslaught, but how to take advantage of the opportunity science presents to broaden Buddhism's view of the universe and of human nature. Would that Christianity were so adaptable.

Made in the USA
San Bernardino, CA
06 March 2013